Out of the Closet and Nothing to Wear

Other Books by Lesléa Newman

NOVELS
Good Enough to Eat
In Every Laugh a Tear
Fat Chance

SHORT-STORY COLLECTIONS
A Letter to Harvey Milk
Secrets
Every Woman's Dream

POETRY COLLECTIONS
Love Me Like You Mean It
Sweet Dark Places
Just Looking for My Shoes

NONFICTION
SomeBODY to Love: A Guide to Loving the Body You Have
*Writing From the Heart: Inspiration and Exercises for Women Who Want to
    Write*

ANTHOLOGIES
*Bubbe Meisehs by Shayneh Maidelehs: Poems by Jewish Granddaughters
    About Our Grandmothers*
Eating Our Hearts Out: Personal Accounts of Women's Relationship to Food
A Loving Testimony: Remembering Loved Ones Lost to AIDS
The Femme Mystique
My Lover Is a Woman: Contemporary Lesbian Love Poems

CHILDREN'S BOOKS
Heather Has Two Mommies
Gloria Goes to Gay Pride
Belinda's Bouquet
Saturday Is Pattyday
Too Far Away to Touch
Remember That

out of the closet
and
nothing to wear

BY **lesléa newman**

alyson
books

LOS ANGELES • NEW YORK

Copyright © 1997 by Lesléa Newman. All rights reserved.

Manufactured in the United States of America.
Printed on acid-free paper.

This trade paperback original is published by Alyson Publications Inc.,
P.O. Box 4371, Los Angeles, California 90078-4371.
Distribution in the United Kingdom by Turnaround Publisher Services Ltd.,
Unit 3 Olympia Trading Estate, Coburg Road, Wood Green,
London N22 6TZ, England.

First edition: June 1997

01 00 99 98 97   10 9 8 7 6 5 4 3 2 1

ISBN 1-55583-415-9

Library of Congress Cataloging-in-Publication Data
Newman, Lesléa.
        Out of the closet and nothing to wear / by Lesléa Newman.
        ISBN 1-55583-415-9 (pbk)
        1. Lesbians—United States—Social life and customs—Fiction.
        2. Humorous stories, American.   I. Title.
PS3564.E91628O96 1997   97-1369
813'.54—dc21   CIP

Credits
An earlier version of "A Femme Shops 'til Her Butch Drops" first appeared in *The
        Femme Mystique,* edited by Lesléa Newman (Alyson Publications, 1995).
An earlier version of "Double Trouble" first appeared in *Dyke Life,* edited by Karla Jay
        (BasicBooks, 1995).
"Have Femme, Will Travel" first appeared in *Ladies, Start Your Engines: Women Writers on
        Cars and the Road,* edited by Elinor Nauen (Faber & Faber, 1996).

Cover design by Bruce Zinda.

For Flash

Contents

Acknowledgments

I'd like to thank Bill Mann and Surina Khan, who in 1993 invited me to write a monthly column for *Metroline*. They are as much to blame as I am for what follows. The editors of the following publications must also be chided for encouraging me: *The Advocate, Bay Windows, Chicago Outlines, Curve* (formerly *Deneuve*), *Dinah, Front Page, Frontiers, Gay People's Chronicle, Gayly Oklahoman, Identity North View, In the Life, Lesbians on the Loose, network, Our Own Community News, Out Front, Q•Voice, Seattle Gay News, Sojourner, Southern Voice, Stonewall, Swagger and Sway, Texas Triangle, Valley Views, Voices, The Washington Blade,* and *Woman Voices.*

I would be remiss if I did not thank my parents and my siblings for teaching me to laugh at myself, as well as the entire Jericho High School class of 1973 for electing me Class Wit, an honor of which I continue to be most proud.

I am grateful to the following people, whose laughter is music to my ears: Tim Duffy, Janet Feld, Tzivia Gover, Roger Grodsky, Jon Hirsch, Judy O'Brien, Marilyn Silberglied-Stewart, Susanna Stein, Mary Vazquez, Susan Waldman, Jess Wells, and Faye and Bucky Wilson.

And finally, I thank the late Victor D'Lugin, whose great gutsy laugh will remain forever in my heart.

My Mother's Move

One Saturday morning Flash and I are in the bathroom unclogging the drain in the bathtub and putting on mascara, respectively, when our mail carrier comes to the door with a registered letter. Neither one of us wants to sign for it. Somehow we both know it isn't Ed McMahon telling us we've finally won the American Family Publishers Sweepstakes. No, it's our landlord telling us he's getting divorced and that he's sure our apartment is the perfect place to live while mending his broken heart.

"That's strange," I say to Flash, mulling over the letter. "Why would a straight man want to live with two lesbians right after his wife leaves him?"

"Honey," Flash breaks it to me gently, "he wants us to move out."

"Move out?" I am stunned. "When?"

Flash reads the fine print. "In sixty days."

Flash and I have very different reactions to our eviction notice. She immediately alerts every liquor store in Lesbianville to start saving boxes. I immediately call my mother. I don't know why. I want sympathy, I suppose. After all, we haven't done anything wrong; our landlord's marriage has fallen apart, and we have to move. But having our apartment, funky as it is, yanked out from under us is more traumatic than I thought it would be. "It's our home," I wail in a voice not unlike a five-year-old's. "I want my mommy."

The trouble is, I don't have a mommy. I have a mother. A mommy gives you milk and cookies, kisses it where it hurts, and makes you feel all better. A mother means well but misses the mark, saying things like "Your room is always here if you need it," as if the twenty years since I've inhabited that room can be dismissed with the wave of a hand.

My mother likes the fact that Flash and I have to move. This is a normal thing that happens to people other than lesbians. This is something we can talk about. Better yet, this is something my mother feels qualified to give me advice about. Never mind the fact that my mother hasn't moved in thirty-four years, ever since my family made the great Jewish migration from Brooklyn to Long Island, and that I, in typical dyke fashion, have lived in forty-three different apartments since 1985. *She* is the expert.

"Have you looked in the paper?" she asks, as if I am an idiot.

"Yes, I've looked in the paper," I answer in my most condescending voice, as if she is an idiot.

"What about calling a Realtor?" she asks.

"Ma, we have to come up with first and last month's rent, a security deposit, and money to pay the movers. We can't afford a Realtor."

This is the opening my mother has been waiting for. "You'll never find anything halfway decent without a Realtor," she tells me. "None of the nice apartments are listed in the paper."

"But didn't you just tell me to look in the paper?" I ask her.

"Oh, you should look," she answers, "but don't expect to find anything."

Weeks pass as Flash and I shlep ourselves all over Lesbianville trying to find a decent apartment. The first time Flash says "What a dump!" with her hips swaying like Bette Davis, I laugh. The thirty-seventh time just isn't funny anymore. Every apartment we inspect has a major flaw. There aren't enough rooms. There are enough rooms, but they're too small. There are enough rooms and they're not too small, but there's no closet space. There are enough rooms and they're not too small and there's plenty of closet space, but there's an electric stove instead of gas and no yard for the cats.

Finally we find an apartment we like, with enough rooms just the right size, plenty of closet space, a gas stove, and a big, sunny yard. The problem is, it's in a bad neighborhood. A very bad neighborhood. What makes it so bad is that my therapist lives right next door. I'd rather move back in with my mother.

With one month down and one to go, Flash and I find an apartment. Not just any apartment. A fabulous apartment. A dream of an apartment, complete with six rooms, wood floors, oak window frames, French doors, two porches, and a yard. I call my mother, feeling smug. All this and without a Realtor too.

"How did you find it?" is the first question she asks.

How did we find it? Flash took a walk after supper one night and bumped into the shortstop on her softball team who had heard from her acupuncturist who had heard from one of her clients that her ex-lover's hairdresser's chiropractor's best friend's therapist had an apartment for rent. In other words, we heard it through the dyke grapevine. Is there even a remote possibility that my mother would understand this? I think not and decide to keep it simple. "Word of mouth," I tell her, and of course she has to have the final say: "I told you not to look in the paper. Was I right or was I right?"

Moving day approaches, and my mother is full of advice. "Pack the dishes first," she tells me.

"Why?" I ask.

"Because it's easier," she says, and I let it go at that since I don't have time to argue.

Packing is a full-time job. Already there are forty-seven cartons stacked floor to ceiling in our bedroom. And those are just my shoes. Finally everything is in boxes, and the movers come and take it all away. Unfortunately, they bring everything to our new place and leave it there for us to unpack. I try to sort out our things while Flash deals with turning on the electricity and the gas, forwarding the mail, and reconnecting the phone. And who is our very first caller? Why, my mother, of course.

What she's calling about surprises me. "What should I get you and Flash for a housewarming present?"

"Ma, you don't have to get us anything."

"I know I don't *have* to get you something," she says. "I *want* to get you something."

"But it's not like we've bought a house or anything," I say, wondering why I am arguing with her. "It's just another apartment."

"It's your first apartment together," she says, and I'm amazed that she knows this. Our last apartment had been Flash's place until I moved in with her, and before that we had both lived alone. This is the first home we've created together, and it does feel different.

"All right," I say and make a joke. "How about a washing machine?"

"Okay," she says, and I almost fall over.

"It was a joke, Ma."

"What joke?" she asks. "Do you need one or not?"

— 4 —

"I don't know — I guess so."

"Fine," she says.

Disbelief makes me brave. "Do we get a dryer too?"

She thinks for a minute. "The washing machine will be your housewarming present, and the dryer will be for Chanukah."

I am floored. This is the closest my mother has ever come to giving Flash and me her blessing. This is the woman who, when I came out to her, called me selfish, self-centered, self-obsessed, and self-absorbed. The same woman who was convinced that I was under the influence of someone because I could never think for myself — or as she put it, "You were always a follower. Why, if they were all walking up Fifth Avenue stark naked with frying pans on their foreheads, you'd be the first in line." This is the woman who never gave up hope that someday I would return to my childhood bedroom and sleep like a virgin in that single bed until Prince Charming arrived to sweep me off my feet. This woman was buying her only daughter and her lover a washer/dryer so that their undershirts and bras, shirts and blouses, pants and panty hose would toss and spin side by side, year in and year out, happily ever after?

Of course, I had to listen to a lecture on spin cycles, bleach dispensers, gas hookups, and the like. Of course, I had to go to Sears, pick out the machines I wanted, write down the numbers, and call them in to my mother for her approval (she picked out a different dryer). Of course, now we have to talk about the washer and dryer every time my mother calls.

"How's the washer?" she asks me.

"Fine," I answer. I mean, how can it be?

"And how's the dryer?"

"Fine." I am tempted to say it had a slight cold last week, but I know better.

"It's drying?"

"It's drying."

"Are you using fabric softener?"

As I listen to her advising me about detergents (after all, she has been a housewife for forty years), all I can think of is, *You've come a long way, Mommy. Thank you.*

Slaves to Love

Flash and I are lying in bed, back to back, feet and tushes touching, like bookends. "Good night," I whisper into the darkness.

"How about a kiss?" my beloved asks.

I roll over to give her a nice, wet smack on the lips and come up with a mouthful of pussy. Now, don't get excited, dear reader. It's not what you think. No, it seems that one of our feline fur balls has burrowed into Flash's neck and intends to spend the night there. And probably will, for Flash and I are love slaves. Not to each other, unfortunately. To our cats.

Now, why is this? I ask myself, usually at 3:00 in the morning when I can't sleep because the cats have stretched themselves out luxuriously on top of the covers and Flash and I are huddled together in a tiny corner of the bed. Flash and I are both strong women. We are childless by choice because we treasure our independence. We like to think we can come and go as we please. Yet if the truth be known, we are completely controlled by our cats.

Of course, our cats are by no means ordinary cats. My cat is a fourteen-year-old femme fatale named Couscous Kerouac (I was going through a vegetarian-beat poet phase when I named her). I found her in a mall in Boulder, Colorado, where I lived at the time. A kid was standing over a box of kittens, and the kid's mother was standing over him, shrieking "I'll drown them, I swear to Gawd I'll drown them" in an unmistakable Long Island accent.

You'd think Couscous would be forever indebted to me, given the fact that I saved her from her fate at the bottom of the Colorado River. But no. Couscous is a brat-cat. She is very, very pretty (which she knows), and this makes people want to pet her. A big mistake. Couscous has to be in the mood, and her moods change as quickly as mine do when I'm PMS. Her purr can change to a growl in two seconds flat, and usually a bite is not far behind.

Consequently, Flash and I fall all over ourselves to please her. "Couscous, want to sit on this towel?" Flash will ask, spreading my very best bath towel from Bloomingdale's across the kitchen floor. "It's hot from the dryer." Whenever Flash or I can get Couscous to sit on our laps for more than two minutes, we gloat in triumph: "See, she loves me." Recently I bought Couscous a black velvet collar studded with rhinestones, which she lets me fasten around her neck on occasion. I tried to convince her to teach a workshop titled "How to Be a Femme Top: A Feline Approach," but she refused. ("Thank God," Flash said. "You don't need any more tricks.")

PC, our other cat, gives new meaning to the word *mellow*. You could pick this cat up and twirl him around by the tail, and his purr wouldn't miss a beat. PC is Flash's cat. Actually, PC, which stands not for personal computer or politically correct but for pussy cat, originally belonged to Flash's ex, who lived on the third floor of her apartment building. One day PC got tired of climbing three flights of stairs, so he just moved in to the first-floor apartment, Flash's place. When the ex moved out, hardly pausing to kiss either Flash or PC good-bye, PC stayed.

I found the two of them years later, a pair of happy bachelors living on Dinty Moore and Hamburger Helper. Couscous and I moved into their bachelor pad, and the four of us became one big happy family. Well, almost. There was a bit of scratching, biting, and yowling at first as Flash and I got used to living together. And we were worried about the cats. The vet said that if they fought, we should spray them with the same perfume to throw off their scent. "Share my Chanel?" I said to Flash. "You've got to be kidding." Happily, the cats decided pretty much from the start to ignore each other and simply get along. Like I said, these are no ordinary cats.

The most remarkable thing about PC is that he is twenty-one years old. Twenty-one *human* years. In cat years this makes him as old as Quentin Crisp and Mother Teresa combined. We did have a close call with PC a few years back when he was only seventeen. The vet thought his kidneys were shutting down and recommended special low-protein cat food, which he happened to sell for two bucks a can. Flash and I brought home a case, and of course PC wouldn't eat it.

"Look, PC," Flash said, scooping some of PC's new food onto a spoon, holding it dangerously close to the mouth that I have been known to kiss, and smacking her lips. "Yum-yum. C'mon, kitty. It's so good." PC and I both looked at Flash as if she had lost her mind. She finally admitted defeat.

I called the vet for advice — and to see if I could get my money back. "Fry it," the vet said. "He'll love it."

Fry it? It's embarrassing to admit, but yes, there I was, standing over the stove, spatula in hand, sautéing a gob of chicken-flavored Science Diet in polyunsaturated fat.

"Hey, what's for supper?" Flash asked, coming into the kitchen. "It smells great."

Of course, PC wasn't so easily fooled. I called the vet again. "Pour some chicken broth over it," he advised. So I went out and bought a chicken.

This time Flash entered the kitchen more cautiously. "Boiled chicken?" she asked. "Are you having trouble with your gallbladder again?" PC wouldn't eat his Science-Diet-drenched-in-broth, of course, but he did enjoy the chicken, both wings and a thigh.

Eventually we went back to PC's favorite food, reasoning that the quality of his life was more important than the quantity. I think he agrees, because four years later he's still going strong. Flash thinks he lives on love, and I agree. I mean, it's not every cat whose owner shleps his favorite chair from room to room all day long, placing it in direct line of whatever window the sun happens to be streaming through (never mind the fact that it used to be my favorite chair). Not every cat has an owner who will sleep in incredibly contorted positions because the cat is taking up three quarters of the pillow ("How in the world did you put your neck out like that?" my chiropractor asks). And how many cat owners will stop in the middle of a big O (feline interruptus) to dash out of the house stark naked because their beloved kitty is yowling from the top of some tree? Not many.

Why do we put up with this? Flash, who has gotten into Zen lately, thinks our cats have lessons to teach us. I got a lesson the other day when I returned home from a three-week book tour. I was feeling pretty full of myself: Audiences had been enthusiastic about my work, and I had been sufficiently wined, dined, and adored. Surely I was on my way to being rich and famous any minute. So why wasn't my family home to greet its rising star? Where were the flowers, the balloons, the champagne? Flash was at work, and the cats were nowhere to be found.

What did greet me at the front door was a puddle of cat puke: Couscous's bulimic revenge. I cleaned up the mess and proceeded straight to the litter box, which very clearly had to be changed. *One minute a standing ovation,* I thought, *the next minute down on my knees scooping out shit.* Was that my lesson?

No, there was more. As I lined the litter box with newspaper, I happened to look down and catch a headline: HEATHER HAS TWO MOMMIES CAUSES WORLD WAR III. And right underneath was a picture of the smiling author, disappearing under mounds of kitty litter. And two seconds later Couscous squatted over my photo to take a pee. I'm still not sure what the lesson is here, but I probably deserve it.

Do or Dye

"Hey, Flash, is this a gray hair?" I ask my beloved, holding a hair straight out from my skull.

"No."

"Are you sure?"

"Yes, I'm sure. That's not gray. That's silver."

That was yesterday. Today when my beloved comes home from work, I corner her again.

"Hey, Flash," I say, pirouetting in front of her. "Notice anything different about me?"

"Let's see. You got new shoes."

"Nope." Good guess though, since I do believe that a day without new shoes is like a day without sunshine. "Guess again."

"You got your nails done."

"Nope. Higher."

Flash raises her eyes. "You got your hair cut."

"Close but no cigar. I got it colored."

"You colored your hair?" Flash is shocked, because I

swore to her I would never do it. What's more, I told my mother I would never do it. But today I did it. I colored my hair.

When my gray streak started coming in on one side, I tried to convince myself that I looked dashingly intellectual, like Susan Sontag, or totally cool, like Bonnie Raitt. Who I really looked like was Cruella de Vil. And I didn't like it one bit.

So off I went to the beauty parlor, as some of us from the '50s still call it. Sitting there, draped in green plastic, with my hair slicked back from my face with black goop, I looked exactly like my mother. Who, I'm sure, would have given anything to be sitting in the next chair over, shaking a red fingernail at me, and saying, "I told you so."

I have no idea how old my mother was when she started dyeing her hair (or "touching it up," as she puts it). She has always had brown hair, as did her own mother, who died completely gray-free at the ripe old age of ninety-nine. "You shouldn't dye your hair. Gray hair is natural," I told my mother way back when, in my adolescent superiority. "Wrinkles are natural too. They give your face character."

"Just you wait," my mother answered, plastering another layer of Noxema onto her cheeks.

So I lived with my gray hairs for a while. I tried to accept them. I really did. I wrote love poems to them. I drew pictures of them. I said affirmations about them. Still, whenever I found one in my hairbrush, freshly yanked out of my skull, I cheered, "Good riddance," and buried it in the trash.

My gray hairs and I tolerated each other for a few months, but then something drastic happened. My twentieth high school reunion arrived, causing me to run straight for the bottle. And thank God I did. Only one poor classmate showed up with salt-and-pepper hair, and believe me, she got dissed but good.

I, on the other hand, made it a point to look fabulous. In addition to my new hair, I got a blood-red manicure and squeezed myself into a black velvet dress cut way above the knee and held up with rhinestone spaghetti straps. I completed my outfit with back-seam hose and three-inch heels. Since I went to high school in New York, where *Heather Has Two Mommies* caused a small war, I figured I was out to the entire class of '73. So since I was out of the closet, I wanted to drag my most dashing attire out as well. Who says a dyke doesn't know how to look fabulous?

Flash wasn't sure she should let me take this on all by myself. "Want me to come along?" she asked, but I declined the offer.

"I love you," I told Flash. "Why would I want to torture you? Unless you really want to spend several hours in a room full of straight people you have nothing in common with."

This time Flash declined. And so I went with Jeremy (Jerry) Fleish, another gay alum, who has been my close friend for twenty-five years (now my age is really showing). Since we both live in Massachusetts (Jeremy in Boston, myself in Lesbianville) and we showed up together, all our classmates assumed we were married.

"Yes, we're married," I said.

"But not to each other," Jeremy added.

"And not the way you think," I augmented.

"But we're very, very happy," Jeremy concluded with a flourish.

"Hello, Petunias." Edward (Eddie) Appelbaum was delighted to see us, especially after I crowned him homecoming queen with a cup and saucer (there was a serious lack of tiaras in the room). Eddie had all the dirt. "She's had more work done than Michael Jackson," he said, pointing to a woman in a skintight maroon jumpsuit. "How do you like Andrea Herschberg as a redhead?" He pointed again. "I bet her snatch doesn't match."

When I called Eddie the day after the reunion, he already had the dish from the night before. "Everyone couldn't get over how fabulous you looked," he told me. A backhanded compliment, but I took it nevertheless.

A week after my reunion, some of Flash's friends from work came over for dinner. "Your hair is such a beautiful shade of brown," one of them said, touching the back of my crowning glory. "Do you color it?"

"Oh, no," I said, jumping out of the way as Flash dropped her beer. I avoided Flash's eyes as I helped her clean up the spill.

After our guests departed, Flash cornered me. "To color your hair is one thing," she said, "but to lie about it is another."

"I don't color my hair," I tried to explain. "I touch it up." Flash's dark eyes flashed. "I only did it once," I pleaded for understanding. "If she'd have said, 'Did you color your hair?' I would have said yes. But she said, 'Do you color your hair?' which means, 'Is it a habit?' You know how literal I am, and I really don't know if I'm going to do it again." Flash wasn't buying, so I changed tactics. "She was rude," I burst out, indignant. "Everyone knows you never ask a lady about her age, her weight, or her hair."

Flash just shook her perfectly shaped head, which, by the way, is covered with thick black curly hair threaded through with glorious bits of silver. Flash has no intention of coloring her hair, but then again, Flash is twelve years older than I am and has already gone through her midlife crisis (lucky Flash — now she gets to go through mine). Flash is not "dyeing" to hold on to her youth the way I am. She is indeed older and wiser. As I someday hope to be.

Double Trouble

"Trash, Flash," I say, reminding my beloved that it is Sunday evening, time to put the cans by the curb. "In a second," she grunts as the starship *Enterprise* zooms across our TV screen. Ten minutes later I plant myself in front of the television, blocking Flash's view of Counselor Troi's cleavage to remind her again. "Next commercial," she promises.

Why, you might ask, don't I just take out the garbage myself? After all, the cans aren't that heavy. But that's not the point. The point is, rubbish patrol is a butch job.

Yes, Flash and I are a bona fide, certified, homogenized butch/femme couple. Contrary to popular belief, butch/femme did not disappear with the beehive hairdos of the '50s. No, we have not changed our lifestyles, only our hairstyles (thank God). Yes, butch/femme is alive and well in the '90s, at least in this household. Only in this household it's femme/butch. Just because Flash wears the pants in this family doesn't mean she's always on top.

So what exactly does this mean? What makes me the femme and Flash the butch? Is it the fact that unlike Flash, I have never been called "sir" once in my entire life? Is it because unlike me, Flash hasn't worn a skirt since 1967, the year she shed her nun's habit? Is it the fact that whenever any dyke in Lesbianville has a job interview or family affair coming up, she runs straight to my closet to pick out a pair of high heels and then begs me to teach her how to walk in them? Is it because whenever Flash and I go out, she steers me around the dance floor with the same smooth confidence she uses to steer our car through New York City traffic?

All of the above is true, but it's not *why* I'm a femme and Flash is a butch. It's just something you're born with. According to family legend, I popped out of the womb, looked at my mother, and uttered the words "Got any mascara?" Baby Flash, on the other hand, was the ultimate tomboy, complete with holes in her jeans and frogs in her pockets. I am thrilled to have found Flash, who truly appreciates the femme that I am, unlike my last girlfriend, who forbade me to wear high heels (except in bed). Flash is the butch of my dreams.

Six years ago, when she was a bachelor, Flash remarked to a buddy, "I'll never find a girlfriend. The only femme left in Lesbianville is Lesléa Newman." When I heard that story, I knew Flash was the girl I would marry.

Sure, you can be a femme without a butch or a butch without a femme, but it isn't nearly as much fun. Flash and I bring out the best in each other. As soon as we started dating, she cut her hair as short as she had always wanted it to be, and I started wearing my skirts tighter and my heels higher. We donned our finest feathers for our butch/femme mating dance. And at our wedding there was never any question as to who would wear a dress and who would wear trousers. As they say in *Glamour Dyke* magazine, "The femme is the picture, the butch is the frame."

Of course, some lesbians think the whole butch/femme thing is, at worst, politically incorrect and, at best, passé. I pity those girls who put personals in the *Lesbianville Ledger* looking for a woman with the qualification "No butches, please." At first I thought they meant "No bitches, please," which I could certainly understand. But when I caught on to what they were really saying, I just couldn't believe it. Don't you know what you're missing, girls? Don't you know that any butch worth her weight in Brylcreem will do anything, and I mean *anything,* to please her femme?

The first time I read a "No butches" personal, I was relieved. At least I could stop worrying that some young lipstick lesbian would pull Flash right out from under me (pun intended). After all, I know a good butch is hard to find.

But then I got mad. How dare anybody underestimate our darling butches after all they've done for us? Because even though we femmes have to put up with straight men coming on to us all the time (and Flash loves knowing that they want me and can't have me), it's my butch that puts herself in danger just by walking out our front door in her freshly pressed trousers, black muscle T-shirt, and short sharp hair combed within an inch of its life. And when Flash and I go out together, it's double trouble. It's obvious that there's something intimate going on between us, though some people aren't quite sure what. We don't look enough alike to be sisters, and Flash is only twelve years older than I am, so she can't be my mother. Whenever we go out to eat, our servers always stumble. Sometimes they'll say, "What'll it be, ladies?" even though Flash is no lady. Other times they'll say, "What can I get you guys?" though I am certainly not a guy. If I were asked for advice, I'm not sure what I'd tell them to say. "Two for lunch, lesbians?" doesn't sound quite right. Nor does "Some dessert for you dykes?"

And so to solve the problem we often eat at home, which means there is a lot of garbage to be taken out. And here it is

8:30, and Counselor Troi is lying prone in sick bay with the lovely Dr. Crusher about to examine her. It would be cruel to disturb Flash at a time like this. And so I decide, just this once, to take out the garbage myself.

No sooner am I back in the house when the phone rings. I pick it up, of course, since I, like most femmes, was born with a Princess phone in my mouth. "Lesléa," my friend Mitzi, who lives next door, is horrified. "Was that *you* taking out the trash?"

"Yes," I admit reluctantly. "Flash is knee-deep in one of her favorite *Star Trek* reruns, and I let her get away with it. But just this once."

"That's a relief," Mitzi says. "I looked out my window and saw you, and my whole take on butch/femme was instantly destroyed."

Not to worry, world. Butch and femme are here to stay.

Meeting Moses

My parents, who live in New York, visit my older brother, who lives in Miami Beach, once a month. My parents have visited me, their only daughter, who lives in Lesbianville, Massachusetts, which is a whole lot closer than Florida, once in the past twelve years. Not that I'd want my parents to drop in on me and Flash every time my period arrives, mind you, but the discrepancy seems a bit extreme. And when my parents did come to see us, it was only because they had a Bar Mitzvah to attend in Connecticut, so they figured they'd come early and drive the extra thirty-five miles to say hello and have a little nosh.

So what does my brother have that I don't have? Besides the obvious — that thing between his legs — and the only slightly less obvious — his six-figure salary — my brother has produced the one thing that has rendered him godlike in my parents eyes forever: a grandchild. And not just any garden-variety type of grandchild — a grand*son*. Since everyone treats the little tyke like God, Flash and I have taken to calling him Moses. Not that we see him that often, since I have visited my brother even fewer times in the past twelve years than my parents have visited me. But my mother, who can't imagine that Flash and I are less than fascinated by every move her heir apparent makes, sends us videotapes every other week so we can monitor his development and growth.

Have you ever sat through a thirty-minute video of a five-month-old infant swaying back and forth in one of those wind-up musical swing things planted on the floor of somebody's kitchen? And I thought David Letterman was boring. "When's the commercial?" Flash asked.

"I don't know, but watch this," I said, pressing the REWIND button for a laugh. But the joke was on me, because the tape looked exactly the same going forward or backward. Even fast-forward wasn't very interesting. I wanted to send my mother a videotape of our two cats snoozing in the sun, but Flash thought that would be rude. Flash also thought it would be rude not to send the little Messiah a birthday present when the occasion arose a few months later and every year thereafter as well.

The first couple of years were easy. Flash and I picked out a tiny playsuit, miniature sneakers, a cute little jacket. Last year, when Moses turned four, Flash said he was getting too old for clothes. "You don't want to be his least favorite aunt, do you?" she asked. "Get him a toy."

"But I don't know what he likes," I whined.

"Guess who does," Flash said, handing me the phone.

So I called my mother, ever the expert, for advice. "He likes cars, trucks, anything with wheels," she said, her voice oozing with pride. God forbid my mother's grandson would like dolls, pocketbooks, anything with rhinestones.

We sent him a set of 100 miniature vehicles, which were a great success with him, though my sister-in-law made it clear in her thank-you note that she didn't appreciate having to pick them up from behind the couch, under the TV stand, and between the stove and refrigerator on a daily basis.

In a move that would make Ms. Behavior proud, my brother, who hadn't called me in three years, dialed my number and put Moses on the phone to say thank you. "Tell Aunt Lesléa how much you like your new cars," my brother said. After a few minutes of garbled baby talk, my brother got back on the phone.

"Wait," I said to him. "Let Moses thank Auntie Flash."

"The rates are really high right now," my brother said, fooling no one since it was Sunday afternoon. "Some other time."

Flash and I finally met our nephew at my mother's sixty-fifth birthday party, which was quite a gala affair. There was enough food to feed all the dykes in Lesbianville and Park Slope combined. There was also a one-woman band, whose rendition of "Sunrise, Sunset" brought tears to everyone's eyes. We sat at a table with my parents and my brother and his wife and, of course, little Moses, who got even more attention than the birthday girl. Every time the one-woman band struck up a tune, he'd ask someone to dance. Flash and I were very impressed by the fact that he didn't seem to care if his partner was male or female, grown-up or child.

"When do you think he'll learn that it's not okay to dance with boys?" I asked Flash, right after a waiter had said to her, "Another beer, sir?"

"With your brother as his father? I'd say before the night is over," Flash replied, taking another bite of chicken Kiev.

"Oh, c'mon, Flash, he's not that bad."

"Wanna bet? Stand up," she said, taking my arm.

"Where are you going?" my brother asked, looking up from his London broil.

"Out there," Flash gestured to the middle of the room.

"To dance?" my brother asked, horrified.

"Sure," Flash said, nodding her head.

"With each other?"

Flash nodded again as my brother dropped his fork. "You're not serious, are you?" he asked, his eyes darting frantically, his complexion instantly pale.

"Cool your jewels, brother. We're just going to the *ladies'* room," Flash said, steering me away from the table. She had proven her point.

A few days later my mother called to discuss the party. "It was such a fabulous affair," she gushed. "And you made quite a hit with your nephew. He just can't stop talking about you. He keeps saying to your brother, 'Aunt Lesléa and Aunt Flash live together, just like Grandma and Grandpa, right?' "

"Smart kid," I said to her. "So what should I get him for his birthday this year?"

"He's very into books right now," my mother said. "He won't go to sleep without two bedtime stories."

"Two, huh?" I asked, relieved that my problem was immediately solved. I didn't have to choose between *Heather Has Two Mommies* and *Gloria Goes to Gay Pride*. I could give him both.

"What do you think?" I asked Flash. "Is Moses old enough for *Heather*?"

"Sure," she said. "Too bad your brother isn't."

Too bad, indeed.

A Femme Shops 'til Her Butch Drops

To shop or not to shop? That is the question one lazy Sunday morning when Flash, the cats, and I are lounging around the breakfast table drinking various forms of cream (straight up or with coffee).

"I can't believe you want to go shopping today," Flash says.

I can't believe she can't believe it. Flash knows my fantasy vacation is a week at Mall of America. Flash knows my all-time favorite movie is *Scenes From a Mall*. Flash knows I always want to go shopping.

"But it's a beautiful day," Flash says, pointing out the window.

I agree. "It's a beautiful day for shopping."

"But you don't need anything." Flash tries a rational approach.

"Yes, I do. I need to shop."

Flash doesn't get it. Butch that she is, Flash doesn't understand a femme's need to run her hands through racks of leather, wool, and silk. Flash gets no thrill from trying on trendy, overpriced, poorly made age-inappropriate garments she has no intention of buying. Flash finds no joy in smoothing different colors of eye shadow along the back of her hand with a tiny brush, looking for just the right shade. But I do.

"I'll make you pancakes," I bargain. "I'll do the dishes after." She's not impressed. "I'll let you have supper in front of the TV tonight."

"It's a deal."

An hour later we arrive at the mall, pull into a space, and I am off, racing through the parking lot with Flash in hot pursuit. "Slow down," she pants, grabbing on to the shoulder strap of my purse like it's a horse's rein. "We've got all day."

"No we don't." I keep up my pace. "The mall closes at 5:00."

"But it's noon."

"My point exactly." I yank open the door to Filene's Basement and rush inside.

Our first stop is the shoe department. "Ooh, look at these." I pick up a pump as Flash groans. "More black shoes? Don't you have, like, seven pairs?"

"No," I say, indignant. I have, like, twenty-seven pairs. I have one-inch heels, two-inch heels, three-inch heels, Cuban heels, platform heels, mules, sling-backs, and slides. I have black heels with ankle straps, black heels with cut-out toes, black heels with ankle straps *and* cut-out toes. I have black heels of velvet, suede, crushed leather, patent leather, and — though I hate to admit it — manmade materials. Not to mention black clogs, flats, sandals, loafers, mules, moccasins, ballerina slippers, Jellies, and cowgirl boots. Flash is right. I guess I don't really *need* another pair of black shoes.

But these are so cute. They're soft leather mini boots with two-inch heels and a heart-shaped zipper on the side. It's love at first sight, and they fit perfectly.

"Are you getting them?" Flash asks.

"I'll have her hold them." I nod toward the salesclerk, and

Flash shakes her head. I have been known to have dozens of salesclerks in different shops hold things for me for hours. Why? It leaves my hands free, which makes it easier to shop.

We leave the shoe department and pass a rack of pants, where Flash picks up a pair of tan chinos identical to the ones she's wearing. "Should I try these on?" she asks.

"Sure," I say, glad she's getting into the swing of things. We head toward the ladies' fitting room but get stuck in a huge traffic jam at the Clinique counter.

"What's going on?" Flash asks.

"They're giving out free gift packages. You get a sample lipstick, eye shadow, comb, body gel, and a cute little carrying case." My voice rises in ecstasy. "Look, all you have to do is buy thirteen dollars of cosmetics."

"How is that free?" Flash wonders out loud.

I know it is useless to explain. "C'mon," I say, elbowing my way up to the counter. I buy a lip pencil and mascara, which I receive along with my free bonus gift in a huge shopping bag.

"Isn't this great?" I am flushed with the excitement of the first purchase. Now the pressure is off; I know I won't go home empty-handed. "Let's go try on your pants."

"Never mind," Flash says as she puts the pants down on a nearby rack. The poor girl is exhausted, but I have just begun to shop.

I drag her across the mall to Steiger's, which is about to go out of business. Everything is at least 40 percent off. I can barely contain myself. My fingers fly through racks of blouses and blazers at breakneck speed. And then I see something across the room that makes me tremble.

A black sweater. Not just any old black sweater. A beaded black sweater. Made of cashmere. With shoulder pads. A sweater's sweater. A dream of a sweater.

Flash states the obvious. "You have a black sweater."

Now, of course I don't have *a* black sweater. I have dozens of black sweaters. I have a scoop-neck, a V-neck, a cowl-neck, a boat-neck, a turtleneck, a crewneck, and an off-the-shoulder. I have a button-down, a backless, one that comes down to my knees, and another that's cropped to show off my navel. I have black sweaters with long sleeves, short sleeves, three-quarter sleeves, and dolman sleeves. I have black sweaters of wool, cotton, cashmere, mohair, velour, ramie, and acrylic. I even have a beaded black sweater. But not like this one.

"Hold please." I give Flash my Clinique bag. "This too." She slips my pocketbook onto her shoulder and groans under its weight as I take off for the dressing room. Once inside, I fling off my blouse and throw it to the floor like some sex-starved maniac. Then I gently ease the sweater off its hanger, slide it onto my body, and turn around to admire my reflection in the mirror. The third button from the top is missing, but that's a minor detail. I am gorgeous.

I leave the dressing room in search of Flash. "What do you think?"

"It's you."

"Really?"

"Of course. Why is one sleeve rolled up?" Flash points to my right arm.

I roll down the cuff and hear a tiny ping as something hits the ground. "Oh, my God," I gasp. "The missing button." Tears fill my eyes. I am unspeakably moved by the kindness of some stranger, no doubt a tried-and-true shopper like myself, who cared enough to keep sweater and button united so that someone other than herself could completely enjoy the garment. Such an act of selfless goodness, especially in this day and age, momentarily stuns me and convinces me that all is right with the world. So much so, that I shush the voice in my head that's telling me to pocket the button, show the sweater's tragic flaw to the salesclerk, and demand another 10 percent off.

"Are we done for the day?" Flash asks, unable to mask the hope in her voice.

"Let me just get those shoes." We head back toward Filene's. "They're perfect for this sweater. All I need is a black skirt."

"Don't you have a black skirt?"

I shake my head, because of course I don't have *a* black skirt. I have many black skirts. A mini, a maxi, a midi, and a mid-calf that's slit halfway up my thigh. A velvet, a rayon, a leather, a suede, and one with three gold buttons going up the side. I also have a black pleated skirt, a skintight skirt, a linen skirt, an A-line skirt, and an itchy wool skirt that my grandmother bought me in 1979.

Of course, when we get home I must try on my new sweater and shoes with all these skirts and various black stockings (opaque, mesh, fishnet, sheer, back-seam, seamless, lace) while Flash watches a *Laverne & Shirley* rerun on TV. During a commercial I pirouette in front of her. "What do you think?"

"Your seams are crooked."

"Fix them." I hike up my skirt, and Flash drops to her knees to check my seams. All of them. Very, very slowly. And carefully. Lucky for us it's an extremely long commercial.

Hours later Flash and I change into our pajamas and crawl into bed exhausted but content. Just like any other typical American family after a day at the mall.

The Belle of the Call

"Hey, Flash, what's a four-letter word ending in *k* that means 'intercourse'?"

"Is that a hint?" my ever-ready girlfriend asks.

"No, I'm doing a crossword puzzle."

"In what? *On Our Backs*?"

"No." I chew on the eraser of my pencil. "The *Times*." I continue filling in the little squares. "It begins with a *t*."

"I know," Flash says.

"What?"

"I'll give you a hint. It's your second favorite activity."

"Talk!" I easily fill in the letters. Of course. I, like most femmes, love to talk. Especially on the telephone.

I have always loved talking on the phone. I was your typical teenager, tying up the phone for hours, sprawled across my bed with my hair in rollers, beauty goop on my face, my right ear glued to the receiver from the minute I got home from school until my mother yelled, "Get off the phone right now and get down here for supper!"

No one else in my family ever stood a chance of receiving a call. Of course, we didn't have call waiting in those days. I love call waiting. My friend Mitzi, who unlike me is not a phone-aholic, calls it "call invading." Whenever we're on the phone and I ask her to hold on because I'm getting another call, she simply hangs up on me. I think that's rude. Of course, Mitzi thinks it's rude of me to say, "Can you hold on a second?" while she's crying her eyes out because she just found out that her randy girlfriend, Randy, kissed someone else while she was away for the weekend.

Maybe I was being just a teensy, tiny bit insensitive. But what can I say? Whenever the phone rings, my heart leaps in anticipation. Who can it be? My agent, telling me she just sold my novel for a fabulous sum? Flash, telling me to meet her at noon for a quickie? Oprah, at long last begging me to be on her show? Of course, it could be a wrong number or — worse — my therapist calling to cancel our appointment or — worse yet — my mother calling to remind me to send Aunt Yenta a birthday card. It could be good news or bad news, but the point is, I've got to know.

On the opposite end of the spectrum from Mitzi is my friend Raven, the queen, and I do mean *queen,* of the telephone. Raven gives such good phone that often while we're talking I will ignore the beep of my call waiting because it's practically a sin to interrupt Raven in the middle of a good dish.

But Raven will interrupt himself. "Aren't you going to get that?" he'll snap. Raven, a true Chatty Cathy like myself, is phone-codependent. He is just as curious as I am to see who's on the other line. Of course, after I finish my second call and click back to Raven, he's gone off on another call himself. Then, while I'm waiting for him to get back, I'll get another call, and in the middle of that call, my call waiting will click, and it'll be Raven, back on the line. So then Raven and I have to talk about everything we just talked about with our other callers.

You have to watch Raven, though. He's tricky. Once in a while I'll hear a click that sounds suspiciously like a Bic pen tapping against the receiver, and he'll say, "Whoops, gotta go." Raven doesn't think I read the papers. He doesn't know that I know there's a new little gadget on the market called "Gotta Go!" which for a mere thirty-five dollars will imitate call waiting whenever you want. The person you're talking to hears a click that sounds like you're getting another call, but you're really not.

When I mentioned this to my mother, she laughed. "I've had that for years," she said. "It's called 'Somebody's at the Door.' And you know what else? I've had conference calling for years too."

"Really?"

"Sure," she says. "It's called the upstairs extension. Hold on, I'll connect your father."

My mother is obviously a woman ahead of her time, but my grandmother is not. The telephone in my grandmother's apartment has been there since the day she moved in, in 1945. It has a rotary dial. The receiver weighs five pounds. The cord is quite short, so that when I talk to my grandmother on the phone, I know she is sitting in the living room on the "telephone chair."

Unlike me, with my light-as-a-feather seventeen-channel cordless telephone with a special attachment (as seen on TV) that Velcros the receiver right onto your head. I could be anywhere while I'm talking to you: in the bathroom shaving my legs, perhaps, or maybe on the back porch working on my tan.

Of course, the advantage my grandmother has over me is that when the phone rings, she knows where to find it. I, on the other hand, have to race around the apartment like a madwoman. "Where's the phone?" I yell as I dash past Flash, trying to remember where I left it: on the back of the toilet? In our closet next to my shoes? In the kitchen behind the microwave? If I don't find it before three rings, the answering machine beats me to it.

Now, here's where I have the advantage over my grandmother. My grandmother doesn't have an answering machine. It took years to convince her to talk to mine. At first she didn't get it. "Who's that answering your phone?" she'd ask.

"It's me, Grandma. I'm talking on a machine."

"So if you're there talking on a machine, why don't you pick up the phone?"

"No, Grandma, it's not really me. I'm not home."

"So if you're not home, who's that stranger answering the phone?"

Of course I *adore* my answering machine. When I walk in the house, Couscous the cat doesn't greet me; instead she jumps onto the answering machine, since she knows that's where I'm heading. I write down all my messages and decide who I'm calling and who I'm not calling back.

This is the downside of having an answering machine. Gone are the good old days when you could simply say, "You called a week ago? Really? My girlfriend never told me." One can only say "My answering machine was broken" or "My cat erased my messages" so many times. Of course, the flip side of this is that you can call people you don't want to talk to when you know they're not going to be home. Simply leave a message when you know they're at work or away for the weekend: "I'm leaving you for Henrietta." Or "I still don't have that 200 bucks. Sorry."

Flash doesn't understand my fascination with the phone. For Flash a phone call is a means to an end: "Wanna go to Angelo's party? I'll pick you up at 7:00."

Now Raven and I, on the other hand, will be on the phone for hours making pre-party plans. "Are you going to Angelo's party? What are you wearing? Skirt or jeans? Glasses or contacts? Do you think Bennett will be there? I think Bennett is so cute. Hold on, I'm getting another call. Okay, I'm back. Angelo says Bennett isn't coming and we should bring drinks. What do you think — wine? White or red? Hang on a second. I'm back, are you there? Mitzi wants us to pick her up. Should she bring her sleazy dress or her sleazy girlfriend? Both? Are you sure? Hold on. I'm back. Angelo says don't forget a corkscrew. Should we go in your car or my car? Should I wear boots or heels? Leather or suede? What time does Angelo's party start? Eight or 8:30? When should we get there? Nine? Ten? Should we go out for drinks first? Where — the Pub or the Bar? Should we ask Mitzi to come or pick her up after?"

In the middle of all this I have a real-life déjà vu experience. In a voice not unlike my mother's, Flash yells, "Get off the phone right now and get out here for supper!"

"Whoops," I say to Raven. "Somebody's at the door. Gotta go!"

I walk out into the kitchen and see that my beloved Flash has set the table with flowers, champagne, and candlesticks. If I play my cards right, we might be in for a little intercourse tonight — you know, the other kind, that doesn't begin with the letter *t*.

I can't wait to call Raven and tell him.

The Show *Must* Go On

When I'm away on a book tour, I call home every night. On a recent Thursday night the conversation went like this:

FLASH: I'm so glad you called! Any word from Michael?

ME: No, not a thing. And not a peep out of Liz either.

FLASH [*moaning*]: What are we gonna do with them?

ME [*imitating my mother*]: I'd like to knock both their heads together.

If anyone had been eavesdropping on our conversation (and chances are high somebody might be since we're both on cordless phones), they would think we were talking about friends of ours: a straight couple run amok, perhaps, or a pair of siblings gone awry. But no, Flash and I are talking about people who really concern us: Michael Jackson and Liz Taylor.

We move on to other topics. "Did you see Madonna's Golden Globes?"

"Globes?" Flash asks. "I thought she only won one."

"I'm not talking about the one she won," I say. "I'm talking about the two that were popping out of her dress."

"Oh, those," Flash says casually, like she hasn't noticed what motherhood has done to Madonna's mammaries.

"So what's the buzz on Chastity and Candace?" I change the subject.

"Oh, that was just a rumor." Flash yawns. "How was your reading tonight?"

"It was good. Listen, we better go, it's 8:59."

"Eight fifty-nine?" There is a slight panic in Flash's voice. "Bye, I love you."

"Love you too. Bye."

As soon as we hang up, I zap on the TV to spend a half hour with my good friends Jerry, George, Elaine, and Kramer. No matter where I am, I can always count on the cast of *Seinfeld* to keep me company from 9:00 to 9:30 on any given Thursday night. Some couples, forced to be apart by time, place, and circumstance, take great comfort in knowing that the same stars are shining above each of their heads every night. Not me. My security lies in the fact that Flash and I, though separated by 500 miles, are both watching the same stars on television. We're laughing at the same jokes. We're muting the same commercials. We are one. And afterward we'll both turn on CNN, hoping for a nice, juicy "Hollywood Minute" featuring Cher, Dolly, or one of our other favorite stars.

Are our lives so mundane that we have to resort to celebrity gossip to spice them up? Perhaps. We prefer to look at it this way: Despite our incredibly exciting lives, Flash and I find room in our hearts to care about those much more fortunate than ourselves.

It hasn't always been like this. I was a normal child, weaned on Pop-Tarts and Saturday morning cartoons. But I went through a long "Kill your television" phase, starting when I was sixteen. Back then television ruled our household. No one was allowed to talk when important shows were on: my mother's soap operas, which my father called her "sap operas" and which she called her "stories," and any sports event that involved a ball and a bat, hoop, or helmet, which were of the utmost importance to my brother.

The television even had its own room: the TV room. No other appliance had its own room. There was no toaster room or blender room. I didn't even have my own room. But the TV room was sacred. Consequently, I refused to enter it. While the rest of my family took their designated places to watch *Leave It to Beaver* and *My Three Sons,* I stubbornly retreated upstairs with a thick Russian novel by Dostoyevsky or Tolstoy. "Come down and watch with us," my parents would plead from the bottom of the stairs. "*The Ed Sullivan Show* is coming on."

"I'm reading," I'd say, and my parents would shake their heads and sigh.

"Where did we go wrong?" they'd mumble, heading back to the TV room as the commercial faded and Ed's theme music came on.

When I finally left home, I was proud to be among the 1.7 percent of the American population who lived sans TV. I lived in this smug fashion for sixteen years, until I met Flash. Flash could not believe I didn't own a TV. Luckily, she discovered my flaw early in our relationship, when she was so sleep-deprived that she was willing to overlook anything. Pretty soon, though, we began spending most of our time at Flash's apartment so she could watch TV. She'd don her headphones, plug herself in to the television set, and watch something called *Cheers* while I curled beside her with *The Selected Poems of Yevtushenko.* But then something happened.

It all started with some celebrity benefit Flash was watching. My eyeballs, as if they had minds of their own, kept leaving the pages of whatever tome I was reading to catch a glimpse of a red sequined gown on the set across the room. "Who's that?" I asked Flash.

"Goldie Hawn."

"What's she saying?"

"Sh. I can't hear."

"Let me hear." I lunged for Flash's headphones, and in an instant I was back among the living. "Ooh, look at Jane Fonda," I crooned. "She hasn't changed a bit. Oh, my God, is that Marilyn Monroe?"

"No, that's Madonna."

"Madonna who?"

Obviously I had a lot of catching up to do. I started watching TV with a vengeance. At first Flash was thrilled that I was part of the human race again, but now I think she's sorry. For you see, Flash has created a monster. The biggest issue in our relationship is who controls the remote. Recently I read about a woman who chopped the thing in half with an ax because her husband's channel surfing finally got to her. I didn't blame her one bit. It was the same week that a man threw his neighbor's CD player out the window because she played Whitney Houston's "I Will Always Love You" one too many times. The moon must have been in Radio Shack.

Anyway, now Flash and I live together as a bona fide two-television family. You'd think that would solve the problem. But no. We both prefer the living room set to the bedroom set, and besides, it's no fun watching television alone. It's a family activity. So Flash tries to convince me to watch those butch shows of hers, *Star Trek* and Discovery Channel specials about the strange mating habits of yellow-bellied spiders. And I try to get her to watch the femme shows, those made-for-TV movies based on real-life stories, with titles like *Seasons of the Heart* and stars like Sally Field.

Once in a while we compromise. I have sat through a few episodes of *Star Trek: The Next Generation* (mostly to see how Counselor Troi was wearing her hair), and, much to her credit, Flash did watch all three Amy Fisher movies with me (we both agreed that Drew Barrymore's portrayal was the best). Flash does have her limits, though; I could not get her to watch *Tears and Laughter: The Joan and Melissa Rivers Story* with me. Thank God for Raven, who was over in two seconds flat with a bag of Chee-tos and two bottles of Dr. Brown's black cherry soda. Now that boy knows how to *live*!

Over the years Flash and I have found some common ground. We both love *Xena: Warrior Princess,* and in fact I like to think of myself as a kindred spirit to our heroine: Lesléa, Worrier Princess. And we both adore cooking shows, though we both hate to cook (we get especially turned-on by the sight of Julia Child slapping a monkfish with her big, strong hands). Priding ourselves on being as politically incorrect as possible, we've been known to take in a beauty pageant on a particularly slow Friday night. We'll both drop everything to watch women's tennis, especially if Martina's playing. We both like a good talk show, like the time Geraldo's topic was "Women Who Name Their Breasts" ("Itsy" and "Bitsy").

And of course, everyone knows we're big *Ellen* fans. If the phone rings at our house between 9:00 and 9:30 on a Wednesday night, we know instantly that either someone has died or that Raven is in a particularly obnoxious mood. We like *Murphy Brown* too and almost any show with strong female characters. And of course, the lesbian shows are our favorites. You know, the reruns that feature couples like Lucy and Ethel, Mary and Rhoda, Laverne and Shirley, Wilma and Betty. Hey, if those gals aren't dykes, I'll eat my subscription to *People.* I mean, they dream together, they scheme together, they laugh together, they cry together, they break up, they process, they make up. And they never have sex. Sounds like half the lesbian couples I know. Including Bert and Ernie.

Ah, well. Flash and I are still waiting for the big lesbian moment to happen on the small screen. Who will be TV's first bona fide butch/femme couple? Xena and Gabrielle? Ellen and Paige? Ellen and Audrey? Murphy Brown and Corky Sherwood Forrest? Miss Babcock and Nanny Fine? And now that Roseanne's mother has come out, will she hit the bars like her daughter did a few seasons back? Surely you remember that infamous Roseanne/Mariel Hemingway kiss, though I've seen more passion between Paul Reiser and Murray when Paul gives the pooch a smooch on *Mad About You.*

Well, that's showbiz. My friends at *Seinfeld* mention us every now and then, but they don't really get it. On one episode Jerry remarked to George that it would be great to be gay. "You move in with your lover," he said, "and you instantly double your wardrobe. Think about it."

No, Jerry, *you* think about it. Can you imagine Flash borrowing my leopard-print spandex miniskirt and a pair of pumps? Or me walking around in her Doc Martens and chinos? I don't think so.

No, it'll be a while before Flash and I see anyone like ourselves on television. The lucky lesbian who's going to direct *The Dykes of Our Lives* is just cutting her milk teeth. That's okay, though. I'm still working on the screenplay for the made-for-TV movie based on actual events called *Leslèa: My Life as a Lesbian.* And we're having a little trouble casting it.

"Tony Randall should play Raven," Flash says to me over brunch.

"Tony Randall? I was thinking of Tom Cruise."

"I want Tom Cruise to play me," Flash says, reaching for the toast.

"I was thinking of k.d. lang for you," I say. After all, since I can't have her for real, that would be the next best thing.

"Who's going to play you?" Flash's inquiring mind wants to know.

"Geena Davis."

"She's too tall."

The phone rings, and of course it's Raven, who can always tell when we're talking about him. "Who do you want to play you," I ask him, "Tony Randall or Tom Cruise?"

"Christian Slater," Raven says. "And I hope Geena Davis is playing you."

"Flash thinks she's too tall."

"Joan Crawford should play Flash," Raven says. "Call me back when you decide."

"She would be good," Flash says. "Or Barbara Stanwyck."

"How about Barbra Streisand?" I say, pouring more coffee. "She was kind of butch in *Yentl*."

"No way," Flash says. "Besides, she'd never cut her nails. Though Amy Irving could play you. Or, I know, how about Fran Drescher? She looks just like you."

"No, listen." Now I'm excited. "I'll play myself. *I* look just like me. You know, like in *The Joan and Melissa Rivers Story*."

"If you play you, there's no way k.d. lang is playing me," Flash says. "There's way too many love scenes."

"Well, I'm certainly not kissing Tom Cruise," I say, "and that's final."

Stay tuned.

Visit From Another Planet

"Flash, brace yourself. The PUs are coming." My poor, unsuspecting girlfriend looks up from her newspaper. "The PUs?" She thinks for a minute. "The politically unbelievable?"

"Correct. Also known as the parental units."

"Your parents are coming?" Flash's voice rises in disbelief. "Why?"

"Why, do I know why?" I ask, already starting to sound like my mother. "They want to see the new apartment."

"Can't we send them pictures?" Flash, ever hopeful, asks.

"No." I sit down with a pen and pad to plan. "Let's see. They're coming Saturday at 1:00. We'll eat lunch from 1:05 to 1:30 and go out to dinner at 6:00, which means we'll have to leave at 5:30." I do some quick math in my head. "That leaves us four hours to kill."

"What should we do with them?" Flash asks as if she's talking about an old pair of shoes she found in the attic.

"We've gotta keep them moving," I say, racking my brain.

"Well, what do they like to do?"

"Besides eat? Not much — gossip and kvetch."

"Gee, sounds like someone I know," Flash says, but I am not amused. Four hours of unstructured time with my parents could be fatal.

"They like to travel," Flash reminds me. "We'll take them sight-seeing. Don't worry."

"I'm not worried," I reassure Flash. "I'm hysterical."

Flash and I spend the next four days cleaning the apartment. We wash and wax the floors. We scrub the walls. We dust behind the TV. We clean out our sock drawers. I rearrange my file cabinets. Flash defrosts the refrigerator. I alphabetize the spices.

Finally the big day arrives. I am up at 6:00, trying on everything in my closet, searching for just the right look: sophisticated enough so I don't reinforce my parents' belief that I am a total failure, yet not too well-off, just in case my father wants to slip me a little cash.

At precisely 1:00 the doorbell rings. "This is so nice," my mother says, waltzing into the apartment. "I can't get over how nice this is." Her voice shows true surprise, giving away her suspicions that we live in a barn. "Honey," she calls to my father, "isn't this nice?"

"Very nice," my father echoes. He is bringing up the rear, shlepping two enormous shopping bags.

"Where's the kitchen?" my mother asks. "You know me, I always head right for the kitchen." Translation: Don't even think about showing me the bedroom.

"This is so nice!" My mother surveys the kitchen, her voice still full of shock. She looks around for two seconds and then announces, "I brought bagels. Let's eat."

I set out plates and silverware, while my mother unpacks enough food to feed all the lesbians on Flash's softball team.

Bagels and cream cheese and lox and egg salad and pound cake and applesauce and cookies. Soon we are all happily munching away. This is the easy part of the visit: We can't talk with our mouths full. Soon all eating stops, and conversation must begin.

"So what's new?" my mother asks. If you didn't know her, you'd think she was expressing an interest in what Flash and I have been up to lately. Not so. She is merely thinking out loud.

"Let's see," my mother says. "You remember the Siplinskys on our block?" She doesn't wait for an answer. "The oldest daughter just had a baby. A girl, I think she had. Was it a girl?" She asks my father.

"A girl or a boy, I don't remember," he replies.

"Anyway, it was healthy, that's all that matters," my mother says. "And what else? Remember Steven Silverberg, he was a year ahead of you? His wife had a breast removed. Cancer. But they think they got it all." She pauses for a sip of coffee. "Oh, and the Greenbergs. You remember them, don't you? The ones on our block with the grass that was always so brown. You remember their grass — it looked just like hay."

This is too much. "Ma, I don't remember the Greenbergs' grass."

"Sure you do," my mother insists. "They live three houses down from us in that split-level. You know. They got aluminum siding last year, I told you."

"So," I pretend interest, "what about the Greenbergs?"

"They got sod."

"They got sod?"

"Yeah, they got sod, can you believe it? Their lawn is gorgeous now."

What in the world can I possibly say to this: The grass is always Greenberg? Flash sees that I am fading fast, so she suggests going for a ride. My parents love riding in the car. It's their favorite form of exercise. We all troop out to my father's Caddie, and as soon as he gets behind the wheel, he starts to sing. His voice is the male equivalent of Edith Bunker's, which doesn't really bother me, but Flash has perfect pitch and can take only so much. To quiet him down, she decides to play tour guide.

"See those mountains to your right?" Flash leans forward and points out my mother's window. "Notice they run east to west, unlike most mountain ranges, which run north to south."

"Isn't that interesting?" my mother says.

I look at Flash, who mouths, *I don't know what I'm talking about.*

Who cares? I mouth back. *Just keep talking.*

We keep my parents occupied until it is time to change for dinner. Then we're back in the car, heading for a restaurant that Flash and I have always wanted to try but have never been able to afford.

My mother orders a curried shrimp dish, my father goes for lamb. I order chicken, and Flash surprises me by ordering the curried shrimp as well. I raise one eyebrow at her; Flash hates curry. Flash flashes me a smile.

Soon our salad and bread arrive. Now I have nothing to fear; there is plenty to talk about. "Oh, is that bread good!" my mother says, smearing a piece with butter. "Do you think it's homemade?"

"The house dressing is excellent," says my father. "It reminds me of that dressing we had in Vermont."

"That was New Hampshire," my mother corrects him as she slaps his hand away from a roll. "Don't fill up on the bread."

"No, I'm sure it was Vermont," my father insists, and for once I am glad for this inane conversation, because sitting right next to us is the entire Lesbianville pride committee. Words like "bisexual" and "transgendered" fly through the air, but luckily, my parents are too busy trying to remember just where they had that salad dressing to notice.

At last our entrées arrive. My mother beams at Flash. "Isn't this delicious?" she says. "This is so good." She pokes my father. "Honey, you don't know what you're missing. Flash," she adds, turning toward my beloved and waving a shrimp, "we made the right choice."

Now I get it. Flash, always the diplomat, has reinforced my mother's opinion of her own good taste. Thankfully, my mother is so focused on her plate, she doesn't notice the gallons of water Flash consumes throughout the longest meal in history.

Finally it's time for dessert. My parents pass: My mother is way too full, and my father is diabetic. I can't eat another thing either, but Flash orders her all-time favorite: flan. Before the waiter puts Flash's flan down on the table, my parents both lift their forks and take a bite. "How is it?" Flash asks politely.

"You'll love it," my mother tells her, taking another nibble. Flash isn't annoyed, though. On the contrary, she's flattered. Now she feels like part of the family.

After my parents drink three cups of coffee each, it is time to go. We drive back to our apartment, but I discourage them from coming inside. "You don't want to get home too late," I tell them. "And there might be traffic."

"Good-bye now." My father shakes Flash's hand and gives me a hug. He doesn't slip me a thing.

"Good-bye, darling." My mother kisses the air around my cheek. "We had such a wonderful time, I'll never get over it."

Neither will I.

PMS: Please Menstruate *Soon!*

Of all the joys of lesbian life, which are much too numerous to mention, there is one I would just as soon live without: the pleasure of two women living together, loving each other, and being PMS at the same time. It is not a pretty picture, believe me. Luckily, I no longer have to worry about this less-than-fabulous situation, because my beloved Flash has tapped into her ancient female wisdom and figured out how to never have her period again. Yes, Flash is the envy of all our baby-boomer and generation-X friends: She has worked hard and achieved menopause. And it's a good thing too, as I have enough premenstrual tension for both of us.

And this is the beauty of being a lesbian: My lover has been through it all before. Only someone who has walked a mile in my mules (in swollen feet, no less) could possibly understand and put up with the monster I become for seven days out of every month.

Sunday (Day One): It is 3:00 A.M. Flash stumbles into the bathroom to find me squatting in the tub, stark naked, scrubbing the hem of the shower curtain with a Brillo pad. "Why are you doing that now?" Flash asks, genuinely curious.

"Because I can't stand the *shmutz* in this house for one more minute," I say, applying all the elbow grease I can muster.

"Why don't you come to bed?" Flash holds out her hand. "The dirt will still be there in the morning."

"Over my dead body," I say, doubling my efforts.

"Somebody's PMS," Flash sing-songs.

"I am not PMS!" I shriek, throwing the Brillo pad at Flash's head. She ducks and goes back to bed, hoping she can get some sleep. She'll need her strength: The fun has just begun.

Monday (Day Two): I am standing at the oven, poking freshly baked oat-bran muffins with a toothpick to see if they're done. Now that the house is cleaner than when my parents came to visit, my nesting instincts have shifted into the realm of nourishment. Flash and I have terrible eating habits, and I am determined to change them. These muffins are a good way to start; supposedly, they have more fiber than our socks. I set the table with soy butter, organic jam, the muffins, and coffee. Flash comes into the kitchen, slumps into a chair, and sips her morning caffeine.

"Have a muffin, dear," I say in my best Donna Reed voice.

"No, thanks," Flash says.

"But breakfast is the most important meal of the day," I remind her.

"I haven't eaten breakfast since 1969," Flash reminds me, as if I haven't noticed that for the past six years the only thing Flash has ingested before noon is coffee and an occasional Flintstones vitamin.

"But I made them for you," I wail, tears gushing from my eyes.

"I'll take one to work and have it for lunch," Flash promises.

"But I want you to eat it *now!*" I shriek, suddenly enraged. I snatch a muffin and hurl it across the room.

Flash grabs her car keys, ducks out the door, and calls, "Have a nice day."

Tuesday (Day Three): Flash comes out of the shower and finds me sitting in my bathrobe on the edge of the bed, the picture of despair. "What's the matter?" she asks cautiously.

"I have nothing to wear," I say.

"Oh, is that all?" Flash is hardly concerned, since she hears this from me at least once a day. "C'mon, I'll help you pick something out." She opens my closet door and does a double take. Hangers, hangers everywhere, as far as the eye can see. With nothing on them. "Honey," Flash says slowly, "what happened to your clothes?"

"They're gone," I say miserably.

"Gone where?" Flash asks.

"To the Salvation Army," I answer. "I got sick of them."

Flash stares at me in amazement. "All of them?" she asks.

"Yes, all of them. Oh, except this." I walk over to my dresser and pull out a skintight black velvet cat-suit I bought on a whim and have never dared wear in public.

Flash makes me put it on and drives us to the Salvation Army. I buy back my entire wardrobe, which, much to my delight, is part of a two-for-one half-price special. "Look at all these fabulous clothes," I exclaim, "and they're going for a song."

Wednesday (Day Four): The alarm goes off, and Flash opens her eyes to find me sprawled on top of the blankets covered in nothing but Saran Wrap, a red rose between my teeth. "In the mood?" she asks. I bat my eyelashes in reply. "Honey, you know I have to get to work." I pout as she ponders. "Tell you what. I'll come home for lunch," she says. "I promise."

But when Flash bounds up the back steps at exactly one minute after noon, she finds me weeping in front of the bathroom mirror. "What's the matter now?" she asks.

"My eyebrows are uneven," I sob, pointing at my reflection. "My forehead is slanted. My nose is off center. My whole face is crooked."

"Don't be ridiculous," Flash says. "You're beautiful." She reaches to take me in her arms.

"Don't touch me," I scream, running from the room. Flash runs after me, waving a white tissue as an offering and a sign of surrender.

Thursday (Day Five): Flash comes home from work to find a stranger sitting on the couch. "Hello," she says. "Have you seen my wife?"

"I am your wife," I say. "How do you like it?" The "it" I am referring to is my hair. Yesterday it was brown and curly and hanging in ringlets to my elbows as usual. Today it is blonde, spiked, and half an inch long, sticking up from my head like the crew cut my brother suffered all through junior high.

"It's a wig, right?" Flash, always the optimist, runs her fingers over my buzz cut.

"You don't like it," I say, the tears, which are never far off, starting to form.

"No, it's cute." Flash tries to muster some enthusiasm. "I've always wanted to do it with a bleached blonde." As soon as the words are out of her mouth, Flash regrets them. I go right for her jugular.

Hours later, after Flash has said 4,357 Hail Lesléas, I forgive her and allow her to take me to the mall, where I discover a whole new world of accessories: hats.

Later that night the full impact of what I've done hits me. Unlike what I did with my clothes, I can't buy back my hair at half price. Flash tries to comfort me. "It'll grow back," she assures me. "Just promise you won't pierce or tattoo anything." I promise, but just to be sure, Flash makes me hand over my cash and credit cards until the week is over.

Friday (Day Six): Things are coming to a head. I've been crying over long-distance commercials and eating chocolate-covered potato chips all morning. There is a blemish on my chin the size and shape of Canada. My breasts are so huge, I've taken to calling them Norm and Gus (short for *enormous* and *humongous*). I paint my nails Deep Slut Red. Suddenly I have an urge to wear white pants even though Memorial Day is months away. I go to my closet, but Flash has put a padlock on it. I try to call her at work, but I can't remember the number. I hang up the phone and drop the receiver on my foot. The only thing left to do is take a nap. I dream I am drowning in a jar of Paul Newman's Sockarooni Spaghetti Sauce.

Saturday (Day Seven): My "friend" arrives (according to my mother, that's what nice girls say). Flash and I are jubilant. We toast my success as if I have just landed a six-figure advance. Now that I am back to being my old lovable self, I apologize to Flash for my behavior. "I'll be better next month," I vow, but she doesn't believe me.

"We've been through this seventy-two times," she reminds me.

"Oh, c'mon," I say. "I'm not always this bad."

"That's true," Flash says. "Sometimes you're a lot worse."

I remind Flash that it's really all her fault. If she would only teach me the secret of menopause, we wouldn't have to go through this every month. But she refuses.

"When you're older," she promises. "You've still got a decade to go."

I hope we both live through it.

Off My Rocker

I am standing in the tchotchke aisle of JCPenney, trying to convince Flash that a teapot shaped like a typewriter is something I cannot live without, when a high-pitched shriek, loud enough to shatter the faux crystal in front of us, pierces our eardrums.

"Poor kid," Flash mumbles.

"Poor mother," I mumble back, making it clear where my sympathy lies.

The shrieks, accompanied by sobs, grow closer and louder. All of a sudden a thigh-high child tears into our aisle, wraps its little arms around Flash, and holds on for dear life. I have to give the kid credit: Flash's leg is the first thing I clutch when I'm scared out of my wits too.

Flash and I look at each other, and then we look down at her brand-new appendage, who is suddenly very quiet. Flash tries to take a step, but the little tot, who upon closer inspection appears to be of the male persuasion, has permanently attached himself to her pant leg with all the stubbornness of Velcro.

"Hey, it's okay," Flash says, stroking his shiny black hair. "Let me pick you up."

"Up." The little boy-toy raises his arms and gazes at Flash with blissful awe, as if she were his own personal messiah. I have seen such a look only once before: It was on Flash's face the night we saw *Angels in America* and she caught a glimpse of Martina in the audience.

Flash picks up the little tyke, who instantly nestles his head into the soft space where her neck meets her shoulder. I am tempted to tap him on the back and say, "Excuse me, *tateleh,* that space is reserved," but I restrain myself. For not only is the little *boychik* in heaven, but so is my beloved Flash. She's rocking back and forth like all women do as soon as a wee one is placed in their arms.

All women except yours truly, that is. I thought that rocking thing was a basic instinct, you know, like someone puts food in your mouth, you swallow. Someone licks the back of your neck, you melt. Someone puts a baby in your arms, you rock. I don't rock. I freeze.

The first time this happened, I was with my friends Sal and Val, who had invited me over to see their new baby, Gal.

"Don't you want to hold her?" they asked, handing me a bundle of blankets with something warm and fuzzy inside.

"What do I do?" I asked.

"Just relax," Sal and Val chorused, seeing that my entire body had stiffened, much like the Tin Man in *The Wizard of Oz* before he squeaks "Oil can!" and gets that lube job from Dorothy.

I tried to relax, I really did. I tried so hard, I got a charley horse. Gal, who was nobody's fool, sensed danger and immediately started screaming her head off. I quickly handed her back to her co-mothers, a little relieved and a little sorry that my nagging suspicions had been confirmed: I have all the maternal instincts of a tennis racket.

Flash, on the other hand, was born to rock. And coo. And cuddle. I watch her and the joy-boy for a while and then clear my throat. "What now, my love?" I ask, but Flash doesn't hear what I say as a question. She takes it as a suggestion and starts singing to her charge with all the passion of a young Frank Sinatra. Flash's rocking turns into a kind of fox-trot as she dances the Boy Wonder up and down the aisles of JCPenney as if neither of them had a care in the world. When they swing my way, I tap the little guy on the shoulder. "May I cut in?" I ask. He takes one look at me and opens his mouth in a howl of terror, as if I am going to do only God knows what to him.

"It's all right," Flash says, comforting her bundle of joy. "Her bark is worse than her bite."

It's time to get serious. "Flash, what are we going to do with him?" I say sternly, as if the child were a puppy and Flash were a child. "We can't keep him. We better bring him to customer service." Now I'm referring to the child as if he were a bedspread that's shrunk in the wash.

"C'mon, J.C.," Flash says. I assume that my lapsed Catholic has named the little darling after the store we found him in and not the Jewish carpenter. We turn up the next aisle only to see Dad darting among the glass-swan barometers, his shiny black hair flying.

"Excuse me," I say, touching his arm. "Is this yours?"

The man falls upon Flash and retrieves his son. "Thank you so much," he calls back, scurrying away. J.C., who is now draped over his father's back like a sack of potatoes, lifts his head to gaze longingly at Flash. They wave like a pair of star-crossed lovers, and then he is gone.

Later that night Flash and I talk baby talk. Do we want one or not? Flash, always the practical one, says there's no way we can afford a kid. And besides, she's already fifty, so it's really up to me. And I've never wanted a child. Though thirty-something years of Jewish heterosexual training has me convinced that my lack of desire to breed means there is something seriously wrong with me.

I decide to bring the issue up in therapy. "Funny you should mention that this week," my therapist says. "I need you to know I'm taking a maternity leave next spring."

"You're pregnant?" I ask, staring at her stomach, which is still as flat as I've always wanted mine to be. "Don't you think you're taking this mirroring thing a little too far?"

She nods thoughtfully, her body already rocking slightly, and asks me how I feel about her being pregnant. Truthfully, I feel like an idiot for paying her a dollar a minute to talk about *her* pregnancy. What about mine?

My therapist suggests I make a list of all the reasons I think I want a baby and bring it in next week. I leave the session happy: I love when she gives me homework. It makes me think I'm getting somewhere.

That night I write my list.

Reasons I want to have a baby:
1. So I'll have someone to take care of me in my old age.
2. So I can dress it up in cute little outfits from JCPenney.
3. To replace P.C., who is now watching over us from pussy cat heaven.
4. So I'll have something new to write about.
5. Because my therapist is having one.

"Pathetic," Flash says, looking over my shoulder.

I return to therapy the following week with a heavy heart. "Do you think these reasons are good enough?" I ask my therapist.

"Why is it so hard for you to accept that you don't want a baby?" As usual, she answers my question with a question.

"Why do *you* want a baby?" I ask, trying to divert her with a question about herself, but it doesn't work.

"Why do you want to know why I want a baby?" She brings the focus back to me.

But two can play at this game. "Why do you want to know why I want to know why you want a baby?"

She doesn't answer. Obviously we are getting nowhere. I glare at my therapist. She sits perfectly still, waiting for me to say something. Then she starts to rock.

"Will you quit doing that?" I yell.

"Doing what?" she asks.

"Rocking! You rock, Flash rocks, everyone rocks but me."

"Our time is just about up," she says, smiling sweetly and extending her hand for my check.

Back home I tell Flash about the session. "I think I know what *zee* problem *iss*," Flash says in her best Dr. Freud imitation. "I'll be right back."

I hear her car pull out of the driveway, leaving me to my own devices. I decide to relax and watch a movie on television, but my only choices are *Rosemary's Baby* and *Mommie Dearest*. Is this a message from the Goddess, telling me that should I decide to have a child, it'll grow up to be a she-devil and write a memoir called *Mommie Queerest*?

As I ponder the situation, Flash returns and banishes me to the bedroom. I hear a lot of clanging and banging going on. Finally I am allowed back into the living room, where my darling Flash has assembled a genuine imitation bentwood rocker just for me. "Try it," she says, quite pleased with herself.

Tentatively I sit. Immediately Couscous jumps into my lap and starts to purr. I lean back. My feet touch the floor. My toes push off.

Problem solved. I rock to my heart's content.

Me and My Gal

Now that it is perfectly clear I am not mommy material, I have a new idea. I want to be a lesbian aunt. Surely there must be a pair of sex- and sleep-deprived lesbian mommies out there who could really use a break. A couple who would be only delighted to lend me their little offspring for an entire afternoon so I can satisfy my craving to play with a child while they satisfy their craving to play with each other.

I look through my phone book and call Sal and Val. "Want me to spend some time with Gal?" I ask.

"We'll be right over," they yell before I have a chance to say, "How about next Thursday?" Luckily, Sal, Val, and Gal live out in the country, and it'll take them about forty minutes to drive into Lesbianville. That'll give me time to de-Gal the house: I have to place our glass-swan barometer out of Gal's reach, hide the latest issue of *On Our Backs,* and, most important of all, convince Flash to take the rest of the day off and play nanny with me.

I call Flash, but as fate would have it, she's not in the office. "Is she on her way home for lunch?" I ask hopefully.

"No," says Flash's boss. "She's out on rounds. She'll be gone most of the day."

In other words, I'm on my own. Which is okay, I guess. It's just that Gal's kind of a tomboy, and that's really Flash's department. You see, Sal and Val were determined that Gal would have the kind of childhood they never got to have. Both of them were forced to wear dresses, play with dolls, and carry little pocketbooks, when what they really wanted to do was wear overalls, play with trucks, and carry little chain saws. Which is pretty much what they do now and what Gal does too.

I turn on *Sesame Street* for inspiration, and before Bert can say "Wanna play with my rubber duckie, Ernie?" the doorbell rings.

"Hi!" Sal and Val chorus. They are incredibly cheerful, like two people who have just won the lottery. "We brought some things," Sal says, "in case Gal needs a snack." She dumps what looks like a week's worth of groceries onto my kitchen table. "Let's see. There's rice cakes, whole wheat bread, organic peanut butter, barley malt-sweetened raspberry jam, tofu Pop-Tarts, ginseng soda — "

"And here's some extra clothes," Val says, unzipping a gym bag that's bigger than the suitcase I pack when I go away for a week. "There's some underwear, undershirts, jeans, sweaters, socks, shorts, shoes, sneakers, a hat, mittens — "

"Mittens?" It's eighty-five degrees out. Why would Gal need mittens? Suddenly I feel a little panicky. Are Sal and Val deserting Gal and running off to start a new child-free life together? And speaking of their darling daughter, where is she?

"Hey, Gal?" I poke my head into the living room. "Gal?"

"Have fun, you two." Sal and Val make a quick exit while I go in search of my pint-size playmate. I hurry through the living room, dining room, and bedroom. "Gal?"

Just as I am about to give up and call the police, I hear a low growl coming from Flash's closet. I fling the door open, and there's Gal with Couscous, the cat who's been known to intimidate full-grown Doberman pinschers with one claw, crouching in the corner, her tail twitching and her hackles raised. All doubts about my maternal instincts instantly vanish as the mama lion in me rears her mighty head and snatches the poor baby away from what is about to become a dangerous situation.

"Did she scare you, honey? Are you all right?" I ask Couscous, inspecting her for bruises. She snarls in reply, swipes at my arm, and draws a bit of blood. "You better stay in the closet," I say, a sentence I swore I'd never utter to anyone. I deposit Couscous on Flash's favorite sweater and go off again in search of Gal.

I find her in the living room. "Books," she says proudly, pointing to the hundred or so volumes she has managed to dump off the shelves onto the floor, including my signed first edition of *Tender Buttons* by Gertrude Stein, which I had hoped to someday sell for a lot of money to retire on.

"Do you want to hear a story, Gal?" I imagine a lazy afternoon in the rocking chair with Gal on my lap, looking at picture books. Dream on, sister. I quickly discover that Gal is a child of the '90s: She has the attention span of a hummingbird on speed. After about half a sentence, she barks "Next!" and pushes each book away, resulting in my stringing together the following: "Once upon a time Mary had a little engine that could huff and puff and blow Daddy's roommate happily ever after."

Whoops. On to the next activity. "Hey, Gal," I say, "want to paint a picture?" I get out the paint Flash and I use to make signs with for Gay Pride Day, and in two seconds flat the walls, the floor, the sofa, and my clothes are covered with bright orange glow-in-the-dark poster paint. What was I thinking? Gal's somehow managed to get a spot shaped like Big Bird on the ceiling, even though she's barely three feet tall.

What next? I rack my brain. "Hey, Gal," I say, "let's string some macaroni necklaces." She dashes into the kitchen, where I lay out some shoelaces and macaroni shells. Thirty seconds later Gal has lost all interest, and the floor is covered with rigatoni, which, I discover, is very slippery and makes an incredibly annoying crunching sound underfoot.

Now what? I feed Gal some carob-coated chickpeas while I try to think. Only twenty-five minutes have passed since Sal and Val made their great escape. What will we do all afternoon? I decide it's time to leave the house before Hurricane Gal can do any more damage. "Hey, Gal," I say, mopping up her spilled strawberry soy-milk, "want to go to the park?"

"Hooray!" she shouts, heading for the front door.

"Wait a minute," I call. Kid or no kid, I am not leaving the house without earrings and a dab of lipstick.

Gal runs into the bedroom to see what's taking me so long. "Ooh, pretty!" She stops in her tracks and stands still for 2.5 seconds, which I'm sure is a world's record. "Me?" she says, pointing to my earrings. "For Gal?"

"You want to wear some earrings?" I ask her. "Let's see what I have for you." I pray that I still have some clip-ons as I open another drawer. Gal visibly swoons at the sight of my rhinestone collection.

Suddenly I see the light. Clearly, in her heart of hearts, Gal is a femme. In their race to combat gender stereotypes, Sal and Val never even considered that their little girl might actually like jewelry, makeup, and, horror of horrors, the color pink. "You poor child," I say as Gal loops a cloisonné necklace over her head. "I bet neither of your mommies has ever shown you how to put eyeliner on straight." Gal shakes her head as her eyes well up with tears. All at once the tempo of the afternoon changes. According to my watch, Gal's moms will be here in three hours, and there's not a moment to lose.

First I give Gal a tour of my closet. She goes straight for my leopard-print platform pumps and the matching pillbox hat. "An excellent choice," I tell her.

Next Gal raids my jewelry box. "Pay attention," I instruct her. "These are zircons, and these are diamonds. Now close your eyes." She does, and I switch the jewelry around. "Which are the diamonds?" I ask. Gal chooses correctly. I reward her with a facial and a complete makeover.

"Pretty," Gal says, staring at herself in the mirror. "Nails?" she asks, pointing at the red tips of my fingers.

"Okay, Gal," I say, getting out my manicure kit. "But you have to sit very, very still for a very, very long time when I'm done so your nails will dry right. You think you can do that?" She nods her head with great enthusiasm. I paint all twenty of her tiny nails and plant her on my bed. "Now you wait there for a few minutes, and then I'll come in to see if you're dry." While Gal's nail polish hardens, I put my books back on their shelves, scrub the walls, and pick a pound of pasta off the kitchen floor. She is still sitting pretty when I go in to check on her half an hour later. "Let me put one more topcoat on," I say, inspecting her nails, "and I'll tell you my favorite story while you're drying. It's called 'Beauty and the Butch.' Once upon a time...."

Just as I am finishing the story, I hear a knock at the door. "Come in," I yell. "We're in the bedroom."

Sal and Val race inside, the afterglow on their faces turning into a look of sheer horror at the sight of their daughter.

"What did you do to her?" Val screams.

"I hope none of that makeup was tested on animals!" Sal yells. She reaches for Gal, who pulls back her hands, shrieking "No!" at the top of her lungs. I notice her tone of voice is identical to mine when Flash comes too close to a brand-new manicure that's not quite dry, and I can't help beaming with pride.

"C'mon, Gal, we're leaving," Sal says, gathering up the food while Val searches for Gal's shoes.

"Don't forget, Gal, we're getting our colors done at the mall next Tuesday," I call from the doorway.

"The mall?" Val and Sal are horrified.

"See?" Gal says, proudly displaying her nails to her moms.

"Don't mess up your polish." I wave to her. "Bye, Gal."

"Bye-bye." Gal waves back happily, her fingers spread carefully, a gal after my very own heart.

There's No Place Like Home

Ah, here we are, just the two of us: my beloved Flash and myself on a much-needed, much-deserved vacation. I'm sure that you, dear reader, are green with envy, picturing me and Flash relaxing on a deserted beach somewhere, strolling along hand in hand, stealing a smooch or two as the sun goes down. Well, get over it, girlfriend. Our vacation does not resemble a United Airlines commercial. In fact, I have never been so stressed out in my entire life.

The tension started weeks ago when we began to plan. First of all, it's very hard for me to get an entire week off from work. My boss is a real bitch. In other words, I work for myself. Most people don't understand why I don't just take a week off or a week and a half, God forbid. The only people who do understand are self-employed masochists like yours truly. We work for ourselves because we are obnoxious, self-absorbed, impossible-to-get-along-with bores who live to work. Case in point: This piece of writing is supposed to be all about being on vacation. So far it is all about being at work. Which gives you some idea of how much fun I am when I'm away from home.

Flash finally convinces my boss to let me have a week off by brandishing her hedge clippers a little too closely to the wires of my fax machine. I get out my date book, and we compare schedules. We can't go during softball season, which takes care of June and July. We can't go when I'm PMS (we learned that lesson the hard way), which cuts out the last week in August. We can't go the first weekend in August because that's Couscous the cat's birthday, and we can't go the second week in August because I have a dentist appointment, which has been booked since 1989. That leaves the third week in August. "Great," says Flash. "We're there." Now, of course, the question is: Where?

Out come the brochures. Now things really start to get tense. Flash has to convince me, a freelance writer who never knows where her next paycheck is coming from, to spend twice as much money as the rent on a hotel room. In other words, I can spend $1,200 to live in one small room for a week instead of $600 to live in six big rooms for a month. Oh, excuse me. Not instead of. In addition to.

Flash solves the problem by finding a small cabin on the coast of Maine. "It's really cheap," Flash points out. "And it's got a kitchenette. We'll hardly spend a penny," she continues. "We won't eat out, except for one nice, romantic dinner. The rest of the time you'll cook." *I'll* cook? I hate to cook. I don't even cook at home. Why would I want to cook on vacation?

Some people say anticipation is half the fun of vacation. For weeks these people pore over brochures, plan their activities, boast to their friends what a great time they're going to have. These people are nuts. Don't they have a life? For weeks before we go away, I am a total wreck. I have to write four columns and three book reviews. I have to proofread the galleys of my new short story collection and compile a list of possible speaking engagements for the fall. I have to contact my publishers, my editors, my agent, my lawyer, my therapist, my hairdresser, my friends — in short, everyone except my parents — so they know where to reach me between August 18th and August 25th. Plus, all those errands I've been putting off for months suddenly seem extremely important; I can't possibly go away without picking up the skirt that's been at the cleaner's since January or before I send Aunt Yenta a thank-you note for the bagel-shaped clock she sent us for our anniversary two years ago this July. Flash watches me run back and forth, her head snapping from left to right to left again, like she's watching one of Martina's tennis matches.

"You see how stressed out you are?" she says. "You need a vacation."

"If I wasn't going on vacation," I growl at her, "I wouldn't be stressed out."

Soon it's time to pack. The experts say to lay out all the clothes you think you'll need and then take half of them. I do the opposite: I lay out all the clothes I think I'll need and then take twice as many. What is the point of being on vacation and going out to your one allotted romantic dinner wearing the right dress and the wrong shoes? That is not my idea of a good time.

In addition to packing our clothes, Flash and I pack beach paraphernalia: beach towels, beach blankets, beach balls, beach chairs, beach umbrellas, boom box, sunscreen, sunblock, sun hat, sunglasses, coolers, canteens, and, just for appearance's sake, a Frisbee.

"Don't forget to take something to read on the beach," Flash reminds me, packing a big, fat novel. I pile up my reading material: *Publishers Weekly, Feminist Bookstore News, Lambda Book Report, The Harvard Gay & Lesbian Review.* Flash just shakes her head, marveling at my ability to leave it all behind and have a great time.

The morning of our departure arrives. Flash loads up the car. Mitzi, who is up early watering her hedges and watching, calls out, "I didn't know you were moving."

Before we leave I give Raven, who is house-sitting for us, last-minute instructions. "Now remember, Couscous likes to be petted on the head in small counterclockwise circles like this," I tell him, demonstrating on his own head. "Not like this." I reverse direction.

"Got it," Raven says.

"And you can eat anything you want, but if you want an egg, you better check it first, you know, by floating it in salt water to see if it's fresh. I think the fresh ones float and the rotten ones sink. Or is it the other way around?"

"I'll figure it out," Raven assures me.

"And don't forget to make sure the stove is off before you go out," I say as Flash hustles me into the car.

"I'm not a total idiot," Raven reminds me, not for the first time.

"I left you a note on the kitchen table," I call as Flash backs us out of the driveway.

"That's my note?" Raven calls, waving. "I thought that was the second draft of your third novel."

At last we arrive at our cozy little — and I do mean *little* — cottage. The place, cute though it may be, is so small that I can sit on the bed, open the refrigerator, and flush the toilet all at the same time. But no matter. Here we are, just the two of us, away from the phones, the faxes, the mail, the stress. What more could a girl want?

Plenty. A mirror for starters so I don't have to look at my reflection in the toaster to make sure my lipstick's on straight. A television, which Flash conveniently forgot to mention does not come with the place. A telephone, though I suppose that's hardly necessary since I already know there's no room service. Flash makes up the bed since there's no housekeeping service either, and we fall into a deep sleep.

The next morning my beloved is up with the birds. "Listen to the ocean," she says. "Smell the fresh air." She looks at me with hunger in her eyes. "What's for breakfast, baby?"

"Pop-Tarts."

"Pop Tarts?"

"Pop-Tarts. Chocolate frosted or brown sugar-cinnamon."

Flash can't hide her disappointment, but being ever hopeful, she asks, "What's for lunch?"

"Ultra Slim-Fast milkshakes. Vanilla or strawberry."

"I'll cook dinner," Flash says. I didn't think it would take her long to catch on.

She leaves and comes back with a bag of three live lobsters.

"You're eating those?" I ask, amazed. Is this the same woman who has a total fit if I even suggest she kill a spider? The same woman who escorts all wayward moths and insects out of our apartment, down three flights of stairs, and then thanks them for visiting? This lifetime member of Greenpeace is going to throw three live creatures into a pot of boiling water? "Poor Moe," I say, keeping a safe distance from the bag, which is crackling ominously. "Poor Larry. Poor Curly."

"Don't you dare name them." Flash glares at me as she puts a pot of water on the stove. I turn away. I can't help it. All of a sudden I feel like I'm married to Son of Sam. When the lobsters are done, I refuse to eat them and dine instead on dinosaur-shaped macaroni and cheese. Neither one of us enjoys our dinner, and we go to sleep without having wild, delicious sex, which, as far as I'm concerned, is the entire purpose of going on vacation in the first place.

Things do get better, though. We stroll along the beach. We collect shells. We swim in the ocean. We make love. We send

Raven and Couscous a postcard every day. And all too soon it's time to depart.

We arrive home safe, sound, and exhausted after our long drive. Raven, who has managed not to burn the house down in our absence, meets us at the door with a 27-pound stack of mail, faxes, newspapers, and phone messages. Just looking at it all makes my shoulders creep up to my ears and my blood pressure rise. I've never been happier. There's no place like home.

A Little Batty

It's Tuesday evening, and my darling Flash is off to the movies. "Are you sure you don't want to see *Interview With the Vampire?*" she asks, shrugging on her jacket.

"I'm very sure," I say, handing her the car keys. "I have no interest in vampires, monsters, bats..."

"Don't you want to see if Tom Cruise is as terrible as everyone says he is?"

"No. Go." I kiss Flash good-bye and show her the door. It's not that I want to get rid of my beloved for good, mind you. It's just that I rarely have a night all to myself alone in our house, and I have big plans: the latest issue of *People*, a brand-new shade of nail polish to try, and a DoveBar with my name on it waiting in the freezer.

I bring my supplies to the living room and settle in. First I separate my toes with cotton balls and dab High Femme Fuchsia on my nails. Then I lay back on the couch with my feet up, the remote control within reach, and *People* nearby. Couscous, seeing by my accoutrements that I am staying put for a while, leaps up onto my belly and settles down into a purring pool of pleasure. Girls, it doesn't get better than this.

I shut my eyes, and just as I start to relax, something whooshes past my head so close, it sideswipes my aura. Couscous sits up at full attention, her ears pinned back close to her head. I follow her dilated pupils up to the ceiling, where something is orbiting the overhead light at 1,000 miles an hour, like a planet on acid. Is it a bird? Is it a plane? No, it's Super *Bat*!

I run shrieking into the bedroom with my arms over my head, leaving a trail of fuchsia-stained cotton balls behind me. I slam the door and then open it a crack to peek out. The bat is still orbiting madly, and Couscous is sitting in the middle of the floor, her head swiveling round and round in full 360-degree turns like Linda Blair in *The Exorcist*. "Run, Cousy, run!" I yell, like Dorothy in *The Wizard of Oz*. I'm afraid the bat, like those creepy flying monkeys I still have nightmares about, will swoop down and carry her off to God knows where. All the horror movies of my childhood converge in my mind. What if this is just the beginning? What if the bats take over like *The Birds*? How will I save myself?

Luckily, the cordless phone is already on its nightly perch: my pillow. I reach for it and then hesitate. Who should I call? How could Flash leave me at a time like this? Why is she watching a horror movie while I'm living one? I could call Sal and Val, but they live a good forty minutes away. Mitzi would be useless, like me. Maybe Raven would come over. He just moved, but if I know Raven, he connected his phone before he even thought about unpacking his blow-dryer and Paul Mitchell hair cream. I dial his new number, and, thank God, it rings.

"Hey, Raven — "

"Hi, doll. Listen, you've got to come over. I just laid the Jackson Pollock contact paper on the pantry shelves, and it is gorgeous."

"Listen, Raven — "

"I lined everything up perfectly. You know it has all those little squiggles..." He sighs with pleasure. "You know, for an anal-retentive Virgo fag like me, this is better than sex. Well, maybe not better but definitely just as good. Well, maybe not just as good but almost. But then again — "

"Raven, will you listen to me?" My voice is as shrill as Fay Wray's in *King Kong*. "What would you do if there were a bat flying around your house?"

He doesn't hesitate. "I'd call Flash. Why?"

"Because there's a bat in my house, and Flash is at the movies. Will you come over?"

"No way. They're delivering my new couch in ten minutes. In fact, I think they just knocked. Call me back."

Now what? There's only one thing left to do: call 911. A cop answers, and I tell him about the bat. "Lady, this line is for emergencies only."

"This *is* an emergency." I grab the dictionary I keep on my night table for those pesky six-syllable words that sometimes sneak their way into my bedtime reading material. "According to *Webster's*," I tell the cop, "an *emergency* is 'a sudden, unexpected occurrence demanding immediate action.'"

He's not impressed. "Call the fire department."

The fire department. Of course! Maybe they'll send a SWAT team. I dial frantically. "Hello!" I say. "I have a bat in my house!"

"Oh, you do, do you?" the fire chief asks, as if I am five years old and have just told him I have a brand-new doll. "What kind of bat?"

Kind? I didn't know they came in kinds. "I'll give you a hint," I say. "Not the kind you play baseball with. Look, will you please just send somebody over?"

"It'll be about twenty minutes."

Thank God! I hang up the phone and call Raven, but his line is busy. Damn. Raven never turns off his call waiting unless he's having phone sex. He's probably sprawled across his new couch talking to some hot young stud about his freshly laid contact paper.

There's nothing to do but wait. I peer out at the bat, which is still orbiting. Couscous has lost all interest and is up on the coffee table, licking the black-and-white puddle that used to be my DoveBar.

Finally I hear sirens racing up the street, and I suddenly realize I have to leave the safety of the bedroom to let the fireman in. I grab the bedspread and drape it over my head, feeling like the bride of Frankenstein. Then I rush downstairs, open the door, and lead the fireman up to the living room. And guess what, folks? No bat. I am dumbfounded. "It was just here a minute ago," I say, almost in tears. "You've got to believe me."

"Oh, I believe you," says the fireman. "They can scrunch up like this." He holds his thumb and forefinger less than an inch apart. "They like to hide. It could be anywhere."

Anywhere? Like in my underwear drawer? This is too much. The fireman clomps around the house in huge rubber boots, shining his flashlight into every nook and cranny. I follow closely behind, clutching my headgear tightly under my chin like Sister Mary Hysteria. But it is no use. The bat has disappeared as completely as my hope for a quiet night at home. There's no way I'm staying in this house with a bat that could be *anywhere.*

"If you see it, call us again," the fireman says, heading out. I close the door behind him, and whoosh! There it is again! I shriek and hit the floor. The fireman is back in two seconds. "You called?" He looks up, sees the bat, and steps over me to get closer. "Now, don't scare it," he whispers. Scare *it*? I remain huddled on the floor underneath the bedspread while the firefighter coaxes the bat. "There, there. C'mon now. No one's gonna hurt you. It's all right. C'mon. Got him!" I pick my head up off the floor and watch as macho man turns to mush. "What a good bat you are," he gushes. "What a sweet bat. What a handsome bat. Oh, look at you. You're just a little batty." He extends his hand. "Want to see it?"

"No!" I hit the floor again. "Just get that thing out of here." The fireman asks for a paper bag, which I give him gladly. At this point I'd give him my grandmother's wedding ring, my entire Barbra Streisand collection, and Flash's treasured leather jacket — anything to get rid of him. Finally he drops the bat into the bag, and the two of them go off into the night to live happily ever after.

As soon as they leave, I call Raven. "I can't believe you didn't come," I yell into the phone.

"I did come. Twice."

"I mean, over here," I say. "A fireman got the bat out."

"Was he cute?"

"No, he was ugly. He had little beady eyes and these gross little wings — "

"I meant the fireman."

"Oh, for God's sake, Raven." I give up and change the subject. "How's the couch?"

"It's gorgeous."

"Is it comfortable?"

"How should I know?"

"Aren't you sitting on it?"

"Oh, no. It's too beautiful to sit on. I'm sitting across the room, looking at it."

"Raven, I gotta go. Flash is home." I hang up the phone just as my beloved comes into the living room.

She picks a fuchsia cotton ball up off the floor and licks her lips. "Blood," she says in her best vampire voice. "I want to suck your blood." She goes for my neck, and I push her away, which is not my usual response.

"What's the matter?"

"Flash, there was a bat in here tonight."

"A bat? What kind of bat?"

"I'll give you a hint. Not the kind I will hit you over the head with if you ever leave me alone in this house again."

"A bat." Flash starts to chuckle. "So what did you do?"

"I called Raven, and then I called the cops."

Flash really starts to laugh now. "Why did you do that?"

"Because," I say, not amused in the least, "for some reason I thought having testicles was a prerequisite for dealing with bats."

"So did a cop come over?"

"No."

Flash looks relieved.

"A fireman did."

"A fireman? No way. I don't believe you."

"Feel this." I place Flash's hand on my chest. She moves it to my right breast. "Not *that*. This." I place her hand over my heart. Even though the bat is long gone, my heart rate is still elevated. I took aerobics classes for three years, and I never got my heart to beat this fast.

But Flash is not impressed. "C'mon, let's go to bed," she says. As soon as her head hits the pillow, Flash falls asleep. I lie awake, fuming.

But the next day I get my revenge. There, on page three of the *Lesbianville Ledger*, a headline blares FIREFIGHTER RESCUES FEMME FROM FEROCIOUS BAT AT 44 AMAZON AVE. The phone rings all day: Femmes call from miles around to offer me sympathy; butches call in to rib Flash. "Scared of a little bat?" they tease her.

"I wasn't home," Flash says.

"Sure," her buddies say.

"Tell them," Flash begs, handing me the phone.

I hesitate. Yes, revenge is sweet, but if I don't defend Flash now, will she protect me when that bat's big brother comes to call? I tell the truth, restoring Flash's butch ego and making our house a safe place once more.

Visit to Another Planet

"Mail call!" Flash bounds up the steps, a stack of letters in her hand. "Look, here's something from your aunt Yenta." She hands me a thick envelope addressed to us in an Old English scrawl. Definitely an invitation. Before I can open it, the phone rings. Somehow I know it's my mother.

"Can you believe your cousin Shmo is getting married?" she asks. "Isn't that something?" Even my mother can't hide the amazement in her voice. My cousin Shmo is, after all, a shmo. "How about this: You and Flash drive here Saturday morning, we all go to Aunt Yenta's Saturday night for supper, and then Sunday we'll go to the wedding. How does that sound?"

Like the weekend from hell, I want to say, but I restrain myself.

"Why can't we just drive to the wedding on Sunday?" Flash asks when I fill her in on the plan.

"Because," I say, "last time we drove to Aunt Yenta's, we mixed up the Garden State Parkway with the New Jersey

Turnpike and wound up in Atlantic City instead of outside Philadelphia, remember?"

"Oh, yeah," Flash remembers now. "I think I won a hundred bucks."

"Well, fork it over." I extend my hand. "We have to buy cousin Shmo and his lovely bride —" I consult the invitation, " — Maria Theresa a wedding present."

On Saturday we arrive at my parents' house with our relationship barely intact. Flash, who believes that fresh air is the key to health, wealth, and happiness, has insisted that the car windows be rolled down for the entire trip, and I have kvetched the whole way about the state of my hair (windblown is not my favorite look). We decide to call a truce and ring my parents' doorbell.

"Just a minute," my mother calls, peering through the peephole to make sure it's us. She deactivates the burglar alarm, hustles us inside, and reactivates it before giving us each a hug. "You must be starving," she says, as if we have walked, instead of driven, 200 miles. "Let's eat."

Flash trots upstairs to wash her hands first. "I better go with her," I say, and my mother nods. Last time Flash went to the bathroom in my parents' house, the silver- and Day-Glo orange-striped wallpaper gave her an instant migraine. And since the entire bathroom is covered in it (including the walls, ceiling, and back of the door), Flash spent over an hour trying to find her way out. This time she closes the door behind us and reaches for the window. "It's so stuffy in here," she says.

"Don't!" I scream. "You'll set off the burglar alarm."

"I don't understand," Flash says, soaping up her hands. "Don't you ever open a window?"

"No," I say, and even though I've explained it to Flash a hundred times, I explain it again.

When I was a child growing up in Brooklyn, we weren't allowed to open the venetian blinds, let alone the windows, in our apartment. "Remember," my mother would hiss, "if you can see them, *they* can see you." *They*, of course, referred to the neighborhood perverts who also lived six floors up and spent their entire lives just waiting to catch a glimpse of me in my junior miss panty girdle and matching Cross Your Heart bra. When we moved to Long Island, the perverts stayed behind but not the thieves. Our house came equipped with a state of the art burglar alarm, which practically goes off if somebody looks at a window, never mind opens one.

"You mean you breathed the same air all through high school?" Flash asks, drying her hands. Then she nods thoughtfully, as if that explains everything.

"Ladies, lunch is on the table," my father yells. We head downstairs, where my mother has set out a small feast of bagels, lox, and about fifty beige Jewish side dishes (gefilte fish, potato kugel, noodle pudding), which all taste alike. Flash gazes longingly at a patch of blue sky, barely visible above the kitchen curtains. "I've got an idea," she says. "Let's eat outside."

"Outside?" my mother asks.

"Outside?" my father asks.

They look at Flash as if she had just suggested we eat suspended from bungee cords over the Grand Canyon. With chopsticks.

"Sure," I say. I, who believe in presenting a united front, back up Flash, even though I give her a good, swift love tap, disguised as a kick in the shins, under the table. "Let's eat outside."

To my amazement, my mother says, "Why not? Everybody make a plate." We circle the table counterclockwise and pile our dishes with food. Then with great ceremony my mother disengages the burglar alarm and opens the back door. We parade outside and plop down on lawn chairs, which groan as if they haven't had to bear human weight in twenty years.

"Isn't this nice?" my mother says as she looks around and spots our neighbors, the Shmendricks, barbecuing in their yard next door. "Yoo-hoo!" My mother waves, and Mrs. Shmendrick waves back.

"Hi, there," Mrs. Shmendrick calls. "We thought you moved years ago. Are those the children?" She and Mr. Shmendrick cross their yard, heading in our direction.

"We're on our way to a wedding," my father calls, hustling us all inside. "Nice to see you." So much for the great outdoors.

Soon we're in my father's car with all the windows rolled up tight, heading for New Jersey.

"Can we get some air in here?" Flash asks.

"Sure," says my father, turning on the air-conditioning full blast.

By the time we get to Aunt Yenta's, Flash is green from my mother's cigarette smoke.

"Hello, hello," Aunt Yenta greets us. "Sit down, you must be starving."

Flash goes to the window and peeks through the blinds for one last look outside before sitting down. "Tell me," she whispers, loud enough for everyone to hear. "Did your father's car have hubcaps on it when we drove up?"

Pandemonium breaks out. Uncle Nebbish calls the cops and uses the speakerphone so we all can hear. "I'd like to report some missing hubcaps," he says.

"Hubcaps?" the cop bellows. "Did anybody die?"

"No, but — "

"What are you, some kind of nebbish?" the cop yells. "Don't bust my chops, mister. Go buy them back tomorrow on Twenty-second Street." He slams down the phone, and so does Uncle Nebbish.

"Remember," Flash hisses, "if *they* can't see you, you can't see them."

"Oh, hush up and eat your boiled chicken," I hiss back.

After supper Aunt Yenta packs us a doggie bag that could easily feed a small extended family of forty-seven and takes us to a nearby hotel. "We'll meet you for breakfast at 8:00," she says, driving off.

Flash and I head for our room. My beloved tries to open the windows, which of course don't open, and then collapses. We are almost too tired and full to frolic, but neither of us can bear the thought of wasting a king-size bed. Afterward, instead of a cigarette, I offer Flash a piece of postcoital sponge cake. She declines and falls into a deep sleep.

The next day as planned, we're downstairs at eight, dressed to the nines. "*Oy vay*, this is terrible, just terrible," Aunt Yenta moans over her French toast.

"What?" I ask.

"*Oy gevalt*, the wedding, the wedding," Uncle Nebbish groans, pushing his pancakes around on his plate.

"Did cousin Shmo get cold feet?" I ask.

"No," my mother says, pointing out the window. "Look, it's going to rain. I told them not to get married outside."

"They're getting married outside?" Flash asks, her ears perking up.

"In her parents' backyard," Aunt Yenta says as she rolls her eyes. "It was Maria Theresa's idea, and Shmo went along with it."

"Wow, he must really be in love." I take a sip of coffee, which is all I have room to ingest after yesterday. "Maybe it'll clear up."

But it doesn't clear up. It starts to drizzle. Then it rains. Then it pours. Then it monsoons. Then it's time to go.

We arrive at the home of Maria Theresa's parents. They've managed to find a tent to rent at the last minute, so we all troop out to inspect it. It is raining so hard, the plastic sides have to be lowered. Flash can't believe it. "There's no air in here," she gasps.

Indeed, the effect is like being trapped, fully clothed, inside a sauna with my entire extended family, including my brother, his wife, and little Moses, who have just arrived. I go to greet them, and my three-inch heels sink two inches into the mud. This makes me very unhappy. It's going to be a long day.

Soon the bride and groom take their place and say their vows. We sit on chairs that have sunk halfway into the mud so that it feels like we're riding a Tilt-A-Whirl. After the bride and groom both say, "I do," half the room yells, "*Mazel tov!*" and half the room yells, "*Mangia!*" And boy, do we eat. Meatballs and matzo balls. Latkes and lasagna. Ravioli and rugelach. It is a true multicultural feast.

After the eating, the dancing begins. The band strikes up an Israeli folk song, and I pull Flash out onto the floor. Since it's a circle dance, we can actually hold hands. Aunt Yenta grabs Flash's other hand and kicks up her heels. "What a gorgeous affair," she gushes, her pocketbook swinging off her elbow and whacking Flash with every joyous step. "Listen," she says to me. "Everybody thinks I'm the maven. The know-it-all," she translates for Flash. "They want to know what to call you."

"Lesléa and Flash," I say.

"No, you know what I mean. Is Flash your friend, your…" Aunt Yenta can't come up with any more alternatives, but I can: lover, wife, partner, significant other, main squeeze… The words spin around my head as we spin around the dance floor. I am touched that she cares, but I have to think fast because, after all, Aunt Yenta is a yenta. Telling her anything is like taking out an ad in *The New York Times*.

"Flash is my beloved companion," I say, and my beloved companion beams at me in approval.

"Beloved companion," Aunt Yenta repeats, twirling off to spread the good news.

Hours later we emerge from the tent. The sky has cleared, and Flash takes huge gulps of air, like someone whose head has been stuck in a plastic dry-cleaning bag for hours. We say our good-byes, file into my father's car, and head for my parents' house.

When we get there, Flash embraces her car like a long-lost lover. "Thanks for everything," she says, unlocking the door.

"Don't you want to come in and change?" my father asks.

"Wait, let me get you some fruit for the trip," my mother says.

"We really have to go," I say, ducking into the car. We drive off, waving, with all the windows rolled down, and for once I don't say a word about it all the way home.

The Butch That I Marry

"Hey, Flash," I whisper to the prone body lying beside me in the dark. "Flash. Flashy. Flash-Flash. Flasheroo. Flashkins. Flashmeister." But it's no use. It's 12:01, and my beloved is fast asleep. I haven't the heart to wake her, even to wish her happy anniversary. Yes, it's been six blissful years since Flash and I became wife and wife, but I remember our wedding as though it were yesterday.

Before the wedding came the proposal, of course. We'd been going out for only two months when Flash got down on one knee and asked, "Will you marry me?"

I got up on two elbows, peered over the side of the bed, and asked, "Where's the ring?"

Flash, having none, quickly looked around her bedroom and offered instead a good-luck onyx stone that she'd had for years. Not the kind of rock I'd hoped for, but I accepted nevertheless and immediately started making lists: people to invite, people not to invite, the menu, the music…

Flash wanted to celebrate our engagement in a different,

more traditional manner, but I pushed her aside. "There's no time for that now," I said, reaching over her back for a pen and pad from the nightstand. "We've got a wedding to plan."

As the weeks passed I kept waiting for Flash to surprise me with an engagement ring. When none appeared, I started dropping hints. I sang "Diamonds Are a Girl's Best Friend" when we showered together. I said "Give me a ring sometime" instead of "Call me later" when Flash left my house for work. When Flash asked if I had plans for Saturday night, I said, "As a matter of fact, I have a previous engagement." All to no avail.

Finally Flash and I took a trip to our local lesbian jeweler to choose our wedding rings. In all the excitement of buying matching bands, the matter of an engagement ring was simply forgotten. Flash wanted us to start wearing our rings right away, but I was stern. "Nothing doing. We can't wear them until we're actually married."

"Can we at least try them on?" Flash asked. We did, and they looked gorgeous. "Let's just wear them out to the car," Flash said, and I relented. "Let's just wear them out to brunch," she said. "Let's just wear them until I take you home." "Let's just wear them while we're doing the nasty."

Needless to say, from that day forth we never removed our rings. Not even when I brought Flash home to meet the folks. You would think that my mother, who notices everything, including the one gray hair in my left eyebrow ("You really should touch that up"), would notice a gold band on the ring finger of her only daughter's left hand and say something about it. Especially since said daughter's new "friend" was wearing an identical ring on her left hand as well. But you see, my family actually invented the "don't ask, don't tell" policy and has been practicing it for years.

Flash was amazed. "You mean, you're not even going to tell them about the wedding?"

"Of course not," I said. "Then I'd have to invite them."

"You're not inviting your parents?" Flash was aghast.

"You're not inviting yours," I reminded her.

"My parents are dead," Flash pointed out, as if that was any kind of excuse. Then her face took on a look of concern. "Who's going to give you away?" she asked.

I didn't hesitate. "My therapist."

"But," Flash said, looking visibly pale, "I thought it was traditional for the femme's family to pay for the wedding."

I kissed her cheek. "You're my family now," I said, throwing my arms around her. Flash was so moved, she didn't know whether to laugh or cry.

In the ensuing months Flash and I met with a printer, a florist, a photographer, a caterer, a bartender, a deejay, a band, a rabbi, a hairdresser, a dressmaker, a shoemaker, and a tailor. We compiled a huge guest list, since, after all, our wedding was going to be *the* social event of the season. But when our caterer informed us that her sliding scale started at twenty-three dollars a plate, we quickly realized who our seventy-five closest friends really were.

Not that any of them bothered to return the little reply card enclosed in their invitation, complete with envelope and LOVE stamp. A week before the wedding, our caterer was tearing out her hair. "You've got to tell me how many guests are coming," she cried. I tried to explain that lesbians think RSVP stands for "respond slowly versus promptly," but she was not amused.

On the morning of the wedding, I went off to have my hair done and my nails polished. At 11:00 I returned home and began to dress. I had just fastened one stocking to my garter belt when the phone rang. Mitzi, who had come over to help, answered. "It's your mother," she whispered, covering the mouthpiece with one hand.

I grabbed the receiver frantically. My mother never calls me on Sunday mornings. "Who died?" I asked.

"No one," she answered. "I just woke up thinking about you, so I decided to call. So what's new?"

"Nothing."

"What are you doing today?"

My mind raced. What could I tell her? I remembered that old fiction-writing adage: I lie in order to tell the truth. I decided to try the opposite and tell the truth in order to lie: "Getting married."

"Very funny."

Phew. I knew she wouldn't believe me. "Listen, Ma, I got some people here. I gotta go," I said, hanging up the phone.

I fastened my other stocking and continued getting dressed. Soon I was covered from head to toe in silk and rhinestones, complete with something old (my grandmother's brooch), something new (my dress), something borrowed (a tampon from Mitzi), and something blue (the string on the tampon).

Flash, who looked stunning in her cream-colored satin shirt and black tuxedo pants, was also having her period. We'd never bled together before and promptly decided that the simultaneous shedding of our uterine walls was a sign from the Goddess that our union was meant to be.

Then before we knew it, the moment had arrived. Flash and I stood under the huppah, her best butch to our right, my dyke of honor to our left. We were surrounded by our loved ones, who all wore their finest: everything from combat boots, cutoff shorts, and nose rings to high heels, velvet gowns, and diamond tiaras. And those were just the boys. The girls wore their best Birkenstocks, drawstring pants, and T-shirts with slogans on them like BUT, MA, SHE *is* MR. RIGHT or MONOGAMY EQUALS MONOTONY, depending on their point of view.

Flash and I faced the rabbi, who started the ceremony by saying that the two of us looked beautiful and very much in love. Of course I started to cry. Then the rabbi started to cry. Then Flash, who is too butch to cry in front of me, never mind before seventy-five of our nearest and dearest, proceeded to have an allergy attack.

When things calmed down, the rabbi continued. Flash and I said our vows, exchanged rings, sipped wine, and kissed. Then the rabbi emptied the wineglass and with great ceremony wrapped it in a napkin and placed it on the floor for Flash to crush. Out of the corner of my eye I caught Mitzi laughing. Later I asked her just what was so funny. "You left the price tag on the bottom of the wineglass," she said, still giggling. "Even from across the room I could see that it was 50 percent off."

"So what?" I asked, indignant. "You think I would let Flash break crystal I paid retail for?"

After we were pronounced butch and bride, the party really went wild. Flash and I were hoisted up on chairs and paraded around for all to see. Our friends toasted us and danced circles around us. The food was so fabulous, even the vegetarians couldn't resist diving into the swan-shaped chopped liver centerpiece. Both wedding cakes (one traditional, the other sugar-, wheat-, and dairy-free) were divine. I tossed my bouquet, and Flash threw my garter. We smiled so much, our faces hurt.

At the end of the day, we drove off to a nearby hotel. I didn't want to take off my wedding dress yet, so Flash worked around it. We fell asleep in each other's arms, and we've slept that way ever since.

I sigh with contentment and look at the clock on the night table. It is now 12:27, and Flash is still deep in dreamland. I decide to let her sleep. There'll be plenty of time to celebrate tomorrow. Maybe I'll even surprise my beloved with breakfast in bed.

But the surprise is on me. When I open my eyes I see a vision of loveliness: Flash, handsome in her silk bathrobe, stands before me holding a breakfast tray. "Happy anniversary," she says, setting the tray down on the bed.

I ooh and aah over the fresh coffee, the bagel and lox, the red rose. "What's this?" I ask, holding up a small gift box.

"Remember the night I proposed to you?" Flash asks. I nod my head dreamily. "I never forgot what you said."

"I said yes."

"No, you didn't." Flash says. "You said, 'Where's the — ' "

"Ring! Oh, my God!" I tear open the box and gasp at the sweetest, most stunning, most beautiful diamond ring I have ever seen. At last, the rock I have always wanted.

"Is it too late to get engaged?" Flash asks.

I grab her by the neck and kiss her in reply. My butch. I think I'll keep her.

My Queer Foot

After a typical lesbian Sunday morning, Flash holds me in her arms, gazes deeply into my eyes, and says those three little words I love to hear: "Let's eat out."

"C'mon!" I throw off the blankets, fling on some clothes from the floor, and race Flash to the car.

Soon we are sitting across from each other at a cozy little table in the window of our favorite restaurant, reading brunch menus. I read my menu from right to left, as if I'm studying Hebrew. But I'm not studying Hebrew. I'm studying prices. Just as I decide to order something that costs $2.99, Flash kicks me under the table. I look up and see her tilt her head slightly to the right. I follow the incline of her forehead with my eyes, gasp, and quickly duck behind my menu.

Candy, Flash's ex, has just walked in, and the hostess is seating her at the table right next to ours. Candy is with her best friend, Honey, who used to go out with Mitzi's new girlfriend, Whit. In other words, my girlfriend's ex-girlfriend's best girlfriend is my best girlfriend's new girlfriend's ex-girlfriend. Even for a town like Lesbianville, where your girlfriend's therapist is often your therapist's girlfriend, this is a bit much.

As I ponder the situation, I hear Flash whisper, "Be nice."

I lower my menu just a tad so Flash can see me roll my eyes. "I'm always nice," I whisper back.

Now Flash rolls her eyes. Flash thinks I dislike Candy. I don't know where in the world she got that idea. I don't dislike Candy. I hate her. But I can't ignore her. Our tables are so close together that the anorexic waitress pouring my coffee can barely squeeze her nonexistent butt between them.

"Hi, Candy," I say, baring my teeth in what a person who didn't know any better would consider a smile.

"Hi." She looks at me and squints, blinded no doubt by the brilliant afterglow shimmering on my face. I consider offering her my sunglasses, but then I see what the problem is: She's trying to remember who I am. She looks at Flash and then smiles. "Oh, hi," she says. "I didn't recognize you."

Why is Candy being ruder than usual this morning? Suddenly I remember that Flash and I left the house in a hurry and that I'm wearing glasses instead of contact lenses, my hair's a mess, and I have on an old shirt of Flash's and a pair of wrinkled jeans. Not my usual attire.

Candy, on the other hand, looks perfect. She's wearing gray slacks and a fuzzy pink sweater. She's even got eyeliner on, for God's sake. Who bothers with makeup on a Sunday morning? Someone with time on her hands. Someone who hasn't spent the last three hours doing what Flash and I have been doing. I smile a real smile now and try to make my afterglow shine even brighter, if that's possible.

Then I turn away. I mean, I can't help feeling just a little bit sorry for Candy. Why is she out on a Sunday morning with her best girlfriend instead of the butch of her dreams? Is it because I'm out with the butch of her dreams? No, Candy's the one that split up with Flash eight years ago, two years before we got together. I suppose, if you really think about it, I should be grateful to her. But I'm not. She broke poor Flash's heart, and that's just another reason to hate her.

"Are you ready to order?" Our waitress is back.

"I'll have the truck driver's special," I say, even though it costs $11.99. "Three eggs, bacon, sausage, ham, grits, pancakes, home fries, toast, juice, coffee, and pie." Flash looks at me, bewildered. I hate eggs. Bacon is against my religion. I've just ordered more food than I usually eat in three days. I shrug as if to say I can't help it. "All those morning acrobatics — I mean, *aerobics* — really gives a girl an appetite." I look over at Candy and wink. "We really put Jane Fonda to shame, if you know what I mean."

Before she can reply, I lower my eyes, lift my coffee cup, and, with pinky extended, take a demure little sip. Then I sigh contentedly, lean back, and cross my right leg over my left. As I do so, the tip of my shoe accidentally knocks against our table. Things go flying, including a pitcher of cream, which leaps into the air as if it has a mind of its own, splattering Candy's pink sweater with a gooey layer of half-and-half.

"Oh, I am so sorry," I say as Candy dabs at her flat chest with a napkin.

"I'll go get a wet cloth," Honey says, scurrying away.

"How did you manage that?" Flash asks, clearly annoyed.

"Oh, don't get upset, Flash," Candy says, still dabbing. "She didn't do it on purpose." Candy reaches down to fish a tissue out of the purse parked on the floor under her chair. "I like your shoes," she says to me as she straightens up. "Do they come in anything smaller than a size ten triple E?"

"What?" I sputter, spewing coffee down the front of my own chest. I glare at Flash, letting my eyes ask the question, *Did you tell her?* Flash shakes her head, but I'm not sure I believe her. One thing is clear, though: Either Flash has told my archenemy how mortified I am by my gigantic feet, or they really are so unbelievably big, she figured it out all by herself. Yes, somehow Candy knows that I don't hate her for her (dirty) blonde hair, blue eyes, ski-slope nose, or slim cheerleader body. No, years of therapy have taken me way beyond all that. I really do love and accept my zaftig body. From the ankles up, that is. I just can't get myself to accept these flat, almost-as-wide-as-they-are-long, scaly, bumpy, bunioned *Guinness Book of World Records* feet.

I never knew there was anything wrong with my feet until the neighborhood kids started making fun of them one summer. All the other kids' feet made distinct toe, instep, and heel imprints on the concrete squares around the pool. My pancake feet left their entire outline for all the world to see.

From that day on I begged my parents for an operation so I could have an arch. I didn't care that it meant breaking every bone in each foot (there are twenty-six). I was determined. Especially after I read that *Oh! Calcutta!* Broadway's first nude musical, was holding auditions and that the only physical trait the director wouldn't put up with was flat feet. "Do you know what a flat-footed actor sounds like walking across the stage?" he asked in an interview I can still quote verbatim more than two decades later.

I take no comfort in knowing that Ingmar Bergman was known to have said, "Even the beautiful have ugly feet." Yeah, right. If Julia Roberts's tootsies are so ugly, why did she marry Lyle Lovett with nothing on them but a dusting of Johnson's baby powder? I am sure no movie star's feet resemble mine, with the possible exception of Donald Duck, whose footprints in the concrete outside Mann's Chinese Theatre match my own perfectly. I know. I took a special trip to Hollywood just to check.

Flash, in an attempt to help me get over my foot complex, once gave me a gift certificate for a pedicure. "I have really ugly feet," I said to the pedicurist.

"Oh, relax," she said, snapping her gum. "Everyone says that. I've seen thousands of feet, and no one's are that bad." Convinced, I removed my shoes. "Wow!" she said, swallowing her Bazooka. "Your feet really are ugly." So much for her tip.

My feet have informed every important, potentially life-altering decision I have ever made. I wouldn't even consider going to a college in any state whose climate dictated the wear ing of sandals. I almost went back in the closet after showing up at my first all-lesbian event — a potluck dinner, of course — because the hostess made everyone take off her shoes. I gave up karate lessons because it was rumored that standing in stances made your feet spread. I never had a child because my mother told me her feet grew an entire size with each pregnancy. And when Flash popped the big question, I almost said no because I swore I would never marry someone whose feet were smaller than mine. Of course, that ruled out 99 percent of the female population, including my beloved, who has perfect size-six feet with arches to rival Baryshnikov's. Flash so smoothly swept me off my Paul Bunyan-size feet, I broke my own rule, a fact I often remind her of whenever she doubts my devotion. I never doubt Flash's devotion, though. Except at times like these.

"Do you ever wish you were still with her?" I whisper to Flash.

"With who?" Flash asks, swiping sausage off my plate.

I roll my eyes to the next table, where Candy is pretending to pick at a blueberry muffin. "With Candy."

"Of course not."

"Do you miss her at all?"

"Nope."

"Not one part of her?"

"Not one part."

I lower my voice even more. "Not even her feet?"

"Her feet?" Flash looks at me.

"Yes, her feet." I hesitate and then ask a question I've been dying to ask for years. "Flash, are Candy's feet prettier than mine?"

Flash just looks at me. "You can't be serious."

"I am serious. C'mon, you can tell me. Are her feet femmier than mine?"

"Honey," Flash shakes her head. "I don't know. I don't remember Candy's feet."

"You don't?" This shocks me. "You don't remember her feet?"

"No."

"You mean to tell me that if we broke up, you wouldn't remember my feet?"

"Don't be silly. Of course I'd remember your feet. Your feet are unforgettable. In a room full of 10,000 feet, I could pick yours out in a heartbeat."

I don't know whether to laugh or cry.

So Many Clocks, So Little Time

"C'mon, Flash, we'll be late for the movie." I point to Aunt Yenta's bagel-shaped clock ticking above the kitchen table. The big hand is on the cream cheese, and the little hand is on the lox. Translation: ten minutes to six and counting.

"One second." Flash is in the bathroom sculpting the back of her head into a perfect DA. Of course, my waist-length locks have been beautifully combed for over an hour, proving my theory correct: The shorter the hair, the longer it takes to coif.

"Two-minute warning," I shout, ducking into my walk-in closet. As long as Flash is up to her elbows in Brylcreem, I might as well change my shoes. I've been having doubts about the compatibility of stirrup pants and platform pumps all day. But as soon as I change my shoes, I change my mind: The shoes are right, the pants are wrong.

"Are you ready?" Flash peeks into my closet, sees me standing there half naked, and decides she has time to water the plants. I emerge in the perfect outfit to wear to a pitch-black movie theater, see Flash cooing to my wandering Jew ("Drink up, Moishe"), and decide I have time to do my nails. Flash finishes with the watering can, sees me polishing my pinkie, and decides she has time for a quick sandwich. I blow-dry my hands, smell bacon frying, and decide I have time to clean out the top drawer of my dresser.

"Aren't you ready yet?" Flash comes into the boudoir only to find me sitting on the bed surrounded by panties, panty girdles, panty hose, G-strings, garters, garter belts, silk stockings, French stockings, fishnet stockings, opaque stockings, bras, bustiers, teddies, camisoles, slips, half-slips, merry widows, my passport, my birth certificate, my last will and testament, a Slinky, and two lucky pennies I've had since 1965. "Why are you cleaning out your dresser now?" Flash asks.

"Because you were making a sandwich," I reply.

"I was only making a sandwich because you were doing your nails," she huffs.

"I was only doing my nails because you were watering the plants," I puff.

"I was only watering the plants because you were changing your clothes," Flash shouts.

"I was only changing my clothes because you were combing your hair," I scream.

"Can't a person take five seconds to comb her hair?" Flash yells.

"Not if those five seconds leave me enough time to change my outfit four times," I shriek. Then I soften. "Oh, never mind. Let's just go." I dump my entire life back into my drawer and let Flash help me on with my coat.

My darling is a little suspicious: It's not like me to abandon an argument that has great potential for developing into a full-blown, rip-roaring, knock-down-drag-out fight. But I restrain myself in the hopes of accomplishing my mission: to get my punctuality-challenged girlfriend out of the house by the time the big hand is on the butter (6:22).

We get into the car, and I pop Melissa Etheridge into the tape deck so Flash won't be tempted to turn on the radio. If she does, she'll hear the deejay announce the correct time: 6:02. Flash has yet to catch on to the fact that not only are all the clocks in the house fast, but each one has a unique time all its own.

Unbeknownst to Flash, our house is divided into time zones. There's BST (bedroom standard time: ten minutes fast), LST (living room standard time: fifteen minutes fast), and KST (kitchen standard time: twenty minutes fast). As far as I can tell, my beloved has yet to realize that on many a Saturday night, after we share a postcoital dish of ice cream in the kitchen at 11:11(my favorite time incidentally, for symmetrical reasons), we retreat back into the bedroom at 11:01. Of course, the 11:00 news doesn't come on until the bedroom clock says ten minutes after, but Flash doesn't seem to notice. Nor does my poor deluded darling realize that it's impossible to leave the house at 6:20 P.M. and arrive at the movies at 6:25, especially when the theater is fifteen miles away. Flash just thinks she's an incredibly good driver.

"What time is it?" Flash asks as she pulls into a parking space.

"Six twenty-five," I say, pointing to my watch. Of course, Flash doesn't know my timepiece is set to bedroom standard time, giving us an extra ten minutes to get out of the car, cross the parking lot, buy our tickets and popcorn, find our seats, remove our coats, and check out the girls. Most people wouldn't need ten minutes to accomplish these tasks, but Flash is easily distracted. Before we get out of the car, she has to comb her hair, fix her collar, and check for any cat hairs caught on her sweater. Once we're out of the car, she has to make sure all the doors are locked, the windows are shut, and the dent I put in the fender a week ago hasn't changed since last time she looked.

As we make our way across the parking lot, Flash stops four times: once to tie her shoe, once to admire a red Bronco she lusts after, and twice to pick up pennies. When we're finally inside the theater, Flash has to search all four pants pockets and all seven jacket pockets for quarters, because the movie costs $5.75 and like most butches she prides herself on always having exact change.

After we buy our tickets, Flash has to look at the movie posters for coming attractions. Then, of course, she loses her ticket and has to search all four pants pockets and all seven jacket pockets until she finds it. Once past the ticket taker, I make a beeline for our seats, since I know Flash will lose at least ten minutes at the çandy counter even though no one else is on line. She has a dozen decisions to make about popcorn: to share or not to share? Small, medium, or large? Buttered or plain? Salted or unsalted? In a bag or a bucket? What about soda? And then I'm sure she'll stop at the water fountain and the bathroom. Flash does not understand that time-honored phrase "Go directly to jail. Do not pass Go. Do not collect $200." No, my girlfriend has elevated tardiness into a high form of art.

I, on the other hand, am a bona fide early bird. This character defect makes me an outsider everywhere I go. Nothing ever starts on time, and every group takes credit for this phenomenon, with a bizarre sense of pride. "We're running on JST [Jewish standard time]." "We're starting at 7:00 FST [feminist standard time]." "I'll meet you at 8:30 QST [queer standard time]." I am the only person on the planet whose internal clock is hopelessly set at NST (neurotic standard time).

One day BF (before Flash) I decided I was going to make a great effort to join the human race and actually arrive somewhere a few minutes late. After all, would it be so terrible to make an entrance? For my tardy debut I picked a performance piece premiering in Lesbianville titled *Viva la Vulva*. I was certain only the coolest dykes in town would attend such an event and that surely none of them would arrive even remotely close to the time of the performance. The show was to start at 9:00 (QST), and I figured I'd arrive at 9:01 or even 9:02. Why not? It was time for me to start living dangerously. The theater was about fifteen minutes away from my house, and I swore I would not get into my car until 8:45.

At 8:30 I already had my coat on and my keys in hand. At 8:32 I started to pace. At 8:34 I broke out into a sweat. At 8:36 my heart started racing. At 8:38 I started hyperventilating so badly, I didn't know if I was about to have a heart attack or an orgasm. By 8:39 I had lifted my left arm to check my watch so many times, I had developed a painful case of carpal tunnel syndrome. At 8:39 and thirty seconds, with my wrist in an Ace bandage, I rushed out of the house in a total panic. I drove as fast as my fifteen-year-old Toyota would go, praying a cop would stop me and give me a ticket so I wouldn't be on time. But no such luck. Where are those cops when you need them? Much to my embarrassment, I arrived at 8:59. Luckily, there was no one around to witness my shame.

Of course, now that Flash and I are joined at the hip, I am no longer on time for anything. But it's a small price to pay for love, I think, as Flash settles down next to me just as the movie begins, unconcerned that she's missed the coming attractions.

After the movie Flash puts on her jacket, walks directly through the parking lot and into the car, drives home without incident, and goes right from the car up the stairs into the house without any delays. Why she is capable of doing this only when we don't have to be at a certain place at a certain time remains a mystery to me.

Once inside, Flash makes herself a midnight snack (really an 11:18 snack, according to kitchen standard time). She gla through the newspaper and calls out, "Hey, don't forget. Tonight we have to change the clocks."

Oh, no. Changing the clocks always makes me hysterical. I try to remain calm. I can handle this. "Fall forward, spring back, right?" I ask.

"Close," Flash says. "Fall back, spring ahead."

"So that means," I say, looking up at the clock, "instead of 11:30, it's really only 10:30. So we just lost an hour, right?"

"Wrong. We just gained an hour." Flash shakes her head. "You poor thing. Why don't you just relax? I'll change the clocks."

"No, I'll do it." I try to sound nonchalant.

"No, no, I insist." Flash starts with the kitchen clock. I follow her from room to room, bemoaning the fact that tomorrow I'll lose the hour I just gained by resetting the clocks back to their respective times. But to my amazement, Flash follows my system to a tee.

"You know about the clocks?" I ask, feeling foolish. I guess it's true: You can fool some of the butches all of the time and all of the butches some of the time, but I've yet to find a time when I can fool my butch.

"Of course I know about the clocks," Flash says. "But if that's what it takes to get you out of the house on time..."

"To get *me* out of the house on time?" I sputter, ready to start a fight. Then I wise up. I'll let it go, at least for now. After all, it doesn't really matter what Flash thinks, as long as the system is working. "Hey, Flash," I say, "thanks for understanding about the clocks."

"No problem," Flash says. "Hey, as long as we've got an extra hour, want to spend it in the bedroom?"

"Sure," I say, reaching for her hand. Like I always say, timing is everything.

Nail Call!

"**N**ews flash!" Flash announces when she gets home from work. "Nail Diamond's in town."

"Who cares?" I don't even look up from the magazine I'm reading. "I hate Neil Diamond."

"Not Neil Diamond. *Nail* Diamond. It's a nail shop. Here." Flash hands me a scrap of paper with an address scrawled on it. "I made you an appointment for a manicure tomorrow at 3:00."

"My hero!" I give Flash the wet, sloppy kiss she deserves. Flash knows how long I've been waiting for a decent nail salon to open around here. She's heard me go on and on about the fabulous salons in my hometown, New York, city of a million broken hearts and ten million broken nails. When I lived in the city that never snoozes, I knew that if I broke a nail anytime, day or night, on any street in Manhattan I could find a place to fix it. These places, with names like Nails R Us and U.S. Nail Service, were always run by Asian women who rarely spoke a word of English, which was fine with me. In fact, I found it very relaxing to sit in front of a little table and let a woman I'd never met before fret and fuss over my hands while muttering softly in a language I couldn't understand. It was the only time in my hectic city-dyke life I ever got to sit still.

Naturally, when I moved to Lesbianville I planned on continuing my once-a-week manicure tradition. I walked up and down the streets of my new little town, but there wasn't a Nail-O-Rama in sight. What's a femme to do? I hit the mall and bought everything I could possibly need for a do-it-yourself manicure: cotton balls, Q-Tips, emery boards, nail files, nail scissors, nail strengtheners, nail clippers, cuticle clippers, cuticle gels, cuticle creams, cuticle cures, polish remover, topcoats, base coats, in-between coats of many colors, and a nail dryer guaranteed to make my nails harder than the finish on my car. I learned how to give good manicure, but it just wasn't the same.

And so when Nail Diamond opened up, I was more than a little excited. I pushed the door open at exactly 3:00 on the day of my appointment and was greeted by a woman with a high ponytail and a low neckline.

"I'm Buff," she said. "Have a seat." I sat down at a little table, closed my eyes, and inhaled deeply. Instantly the stench of all those chemicals soothed my tired soul. Buff sat across from me and reached for my hands. "Let's see," she said. "Oh, a wedding band. How long have you been married?"

"Six years."

"What does your husband do?"

Ooh, trick question. Luckily, like most dykes, I learned to master the fine art of pronoun avoidance a long time ago. And luckier still, I married a woman with a name that swings both ways. "Flash works for the city," I said as Buff dunked my left hand into a bowl of clear liquid that looked an awful lot like Palmolive.

"I got divorced a year ago," Buff said, whipping out her nail file. "Men. Scum of the earth, if you ask me." She began shaping the nails on my right hand. "I just started dating, and you know, it's high school all over again. All they want is one damn thing." Buff started filing my nails with a vengeance. "They take you out, they buy you a drink, and they think they're entitled to a good time. And you know what they mean by a good time: wham, bam, thank you, ma'am."

"Ouch!" I pulled my hand away from Buff, who, distracted by her tirade, had filed my nail down to the quick and taken a good half inch of skin off the tip of my finger besides.

"That too short? Sorry. We'll put a tip on it." Buff reached for my hand again, and I reluctantly gave it back. Somehow this wasn't turning out to be as relaxing as I'd remembered. Buff finished my right hand, reached for my left, and noticed my wedding band again. "Six years, huh? That's five years more than I lasted. All my girlfriends are divorced. Me and my girlfriend just went out last night, and she told me her husband's leaving her after sixteen years. Sixteen years, Christ!"

"Lovely day, isn't it?" I asked, trying to steer Buff onto a more neutral topic, since she had just picked up a pair of very sharp-looking cuticle clippers. I mean, I like a blood-red manicure as much as the next girl, but she was beginning to scare me.

Buff quieted down, and as she began to clip, I pondered the word *girlfriend*. Clearly to a straight woman like Buff, *girlfriend* meant any number of gal pals like herself who enjoyed sharing a beer and complaining about their menfolk. On the other hand, to a femme like me, *girlfriend* means one particularly handsome butch who knows how to take me to heights of sexual ecstasy I never dreamed possible. The writer in me finds this all quite interesting. But Buff didn't leave me alone with my thoughts for very long. As soon as she started applying my base coat, she noticed my wedding ring yet again.

"So what's the secret?" she asked.

"What secret?"

"The secret to your marriage. What's so special about *your* husband?" She asked the question with such a sneer, I decided to take it on like the challenge she meant it to be.

I leaned in toward Buff as if I were about to share my most intimate secret with her, as indeed I was. "My husband," I hissed the first syllable of the word, "has a vagina."

"What?" Buff dropped my hand, not in horror, it turns out, but in fascination. "You're gay?" she asked, leaning forward again. "Wow, I can't believe it. My girlfriend and I were just talking about this. We wish we were gay. We'd love to be gay. Who needs men?" She gestured with her little brush, which dripped nail polish all over the carpet, but Buff didn't seem to care. "So tell me," Buff said, her voice dropping to an intimate whisper, "did you ever date guys, or were you always gay? When did you know? Is the sex better?"

I don't believe this. All I wanted was a manicure, and instead there I was, about to give a lesson in Lesbianism 101. *I shouldn't be paying Buff,* I thought, *Buff should be paying me.*

She went on: "I love my girlfriend, I really do. I mean, we do everything together. We do each other's nails, we borrow each other's clothes, we cook for each other, we talk on the phone for hours. But sex? I don't know if that would work."

Of course it wouldn't work. You're both femmes, I wanted to scream. But somehow I knew Buff wasn't ready for an advanced lesson on butch/femme dynamics at this point. "Isn't it time for me to choose a color?" I asked Buff, who seemed to have forgotten why I was there in the first place.

"Oh, yeah." Buff displayed her polish: Cracklin' Rosie; Red, Red Wine; Cherry Cherry; Song Sung Blue; Sweet Caroline… All the colors were named after Neil Diamond songs. Neil Diamond, Nail Diamond. I complimented Buff on her cleverness.

"You gotta have a gimmick," she said, opening a bottle of Heartlight. "You know, when I moved to this town, I thought, *Piece of cake, plenty of women,* but business has been really slow. For some reason most of the women in this town keep their nails awfully short."

There was a questioning tone to her voice, but if Buff couldn't figure out why most of the citizens of Lesbianville didn't do well with long pointed nails, I certainly was not going to tell her. Instead, I decided to give her a little hint. "Did you see *Go Fish?*" I asked. "It's this movie about two women who fall in love, and there's this great nail clippers scene at the end of the film. I think you'd really like it."

"I'll have to check that out." Buff applied a topcoat to my nails.

I was almost dry when the door of the salon opened, and who walked in but my beloved Flash.

"How's it going?" she asked.

"Fine," I lied. For once, Buff was speechless. Flash tends to have this effect on lesbian wanna-bes. "Buff, this is Flash," I said.

Buff shook her head as if she were coming out of a trance and walked toward Flash, her cleavage leading the way, her hips swaying from side to side. "How do you do?" she asked in a husky voice. I was tempted to scratch her eyes out, but my nails weren't quite dry.

"Flash, my love, can you pay Buff?" I asked, staking out my territory. A straight woman like Buff would surely know that anyone who paid to have my nails shaped and polished belonged to me. Till death do us part.

Flash fished some money out of her pocket, dropped it into my lap, and, smelling a catfight, quickly took her leave.

"Nice to meet you," Buff said, waving from the doorway. "Come back anytime." She stood still for a moment, mesmerized by Flash's retreating shadow, and then turned back to me.

"Got any more like that at home?" she asked. "If I ever met a woman like that, I'd turn gay in a heartbeat."

All it takes is one good butch, I thought, *but that good butch is taken.* And on that note I left Nail Diamond without looking back.

"But why?" Flash asked when I got home. "She seemed nice enough, and your nails look great."

"Because she has a huge crush on you."

"Oh, c'mon," Flash said. "She's hardly my type. Let's just find someone to bring her out."

"Who?" I started thinking out loud. "Sal and Val are taken. Mitzi and Whit are still an item. Raven has the wrong plumbing. Oh, well. I guess poor Buff is on her own." And in the meantime, just in case, I'm sharpening my claws at home.

Our Pocketbooks, Ourselves

I must be dreaming. It's a beautiful Saturday morning, and I could swear Flash just said, "Want to go to the mall?" I must have heard wrong, like that time in sixth grade when I thought my teacher was talking about the Great Mall of China. I don't think I could live through such disappointment again. Maybe Flash wants me to accompany her into the hall or out to a ball. Feigning indifference, I cautiously ask, "What did you say, dear?"

"I said, 'Want to go to the mall?' You know, that new place, Mall of Your Dreams, is opening. But if you don't think it's a good idea..."

"Hey, you don't have to ask me twice." I grab my pocketbook before my beloved can grab hold of her senses. "Let's go."

Soon we're in the car, seated next to each other, zipping down the highway. I futz with the radio and settle on an oldies station. Just as I sit back, Flash starts jerking about in her seat, thrashing frantically from side to side. "What in the world are you doing?" I ask her. "No, don't tell me. Let me guess." I study my beloved, snapping my fingers to the beat. "The watusi? The jerk? The twist?"

"I'm just trying to get a tissue out of my pocket." Flash slides her hand under her seat belt, snakes two fingers into her pocket, and thrusts her hips up into the air as if she's about to have wild sex with the steering wheel.

"Here." I bend down for my pocketbook just as the car swerves to the left, narrowly missing a green Volvo.

Flash's fingers emerge from her pocket, clinging to two thirds of a Kleenex. "Don't bother," she says, steering the car back onto the road. "I got it."

Strange as it may seem, Flash would rather endanger both our lives than carry a pocketbook. This amazes me. I don't care how butch a woman is; I don't understand how she can go through life without a purse.

I remember my first pocketbook the way most girls remember their first kiss. My mother, who for years had heard me whine "I want a pocketbook just like yours," went out and bought us matching gold lamé shoulder bags decorated with leopard-print patches.

"What's the matter, you don't like them?" she asked, surprised at the look of horror on my face. "They were on sale, a two-for-one special. What's not to like?"

My grandmother offered to buy me a pocketbook just like hers, but her handbag was made of straw and decorated with huge turquoise and magenta flowers and the words MIAMI BEACH spelled out in seashells along the strap. Not only that, but it doubled as a sun hat when emptied out and turned upside down. My grandmother loved that bag so much, she still had it with her when she went into a nursing home at the age of ninety-nine.

"Why does she need her pocketbook?" Flash wanted to know. "She's not going anywhere."

I patiently explained to my poor, ignorant spouse that my grandmother needed her pocketbook "just in case."

"Just in case of what?" Flash asked.

"Just in case she gets a headache and she needs an aspirin," I said. "Just in case she wants to play gin rummy and she needs a deck of cards. Just in case someone gets fresh with her and she needs to hit him over the head. Just in case she's sitting outside in the sun and she needs to put on a hat."

I still have my first pocketbook and all the other bags I've shlepped around through various phases of my life. In my teenage years, as an act of rebellion, I carried around a pair of denim shorts with the legs sewn shut and a belt attached as a shoulder strap (and you Generation X dykes thought *you* invented grunge). In my holier-than-thou, back-to-the-earth hippie days, I dragged around a canvas Save-a-Tree bag decorated with buttons: SAVE WATER, SHOWER WITH A FRIEND; SAVE THE WHALES; SAVE GREEN STAMPS. In my artsy-fartsy days I actually made pocketbooks by pasting magazine pictures onto old-fashioned metal lunch pails and covering them with shellac. I thought they were a steal at twenty-five bucks (too bad nobody else did). When I came out as a lesbian feminist, I carried a no-nonsense book bag that held a can of mace. When I came out as a lesbian femme, I started to carry a sweet little purse with an extra pair of No Nonsense panty hose decorated with lace.

Over the years my pocketbook collection has grown to include handbags, shoulder bags, silk bags, suede bags, purses, pouches, and clutches. I have bags decorated with pearls, rhinestones, sequins, fringe, mesh, beads, and macramé. I have a backpack, a fanny pack, a purse that attaches to my belt, and something called a "wallet on a string." Today, in honor of our excursion to the new mall in town, I am sporting my favorite everyday bag: a basic black tote that is so huge, Flash has christened it "Montana."

We turn into the mall and see, much to our dismay, that the parking lot is full. Up and down the rows we go. Finally I spot a woman carrying a small white bag (even though it is way past Labor Day), keys dangling from her fingers.

"Follow that clutch!" I yell. "And step on it." Flash just looks at me, and then I remember: My beloved thinks a clutch is part of a car, not a pocketbook without straps. "Follow her!" I point to the woman walking ahead of us. "She's got keys in her hand."

We crawl along behind the woman for an eternity, down to the end of an aisle. "Where the hell did she park?" Flash asks, as if I know. Suddenly the woman turns left and cuts two rows over. "Shit," Flash mutters. "Now what?"

"Catch her," I yell, jumping out of the car in hot pursuit.

The woman gets into her car and backs out, just as a blue Buick pulls up, its blinker blinking to beat the band. I leap into the now-vacated spot and stand my ground. "Hurry, Flash!" I yell as my beloved turns the corner.

"Get out of that damn spot!" the driver of the Buick screams, brandishing his fist.

"You'll have to kill me first," I scream back, brandishing my pocketbook, which can be used as a deadly weapon if necessary. The poor guy sees he has met his match and peals out, tires squealing. I step aside and wave Flash into the space.

"Do me a favor," Flash says. "Don't try that in New York."

"Where do you think I learned it?" I ask.

She just shakes her head and gathers up her things. Her wallet's in the glove compartment, her comb's in the visor, and her credit cards are on the dash. "Can you hold these?" Flash asks, handing me her keys, her wallet, her credit cards, a comb, some tissues, and a pair of heavy socks in case she tries on some shoes.

"No problem." I stuff Flash's stuff in with my stuff, which includes my change purse, my checkbook, my address book, my notebook, pens, Scotch tape, and stamps. And that's only one of six compartments. Behind door number two we have lipstick, ChapStick, mascara, blush, a hairbrush, hair spray, and mousse. Compartment number three holds a toothbrush, dental floss, gum, gumdrops, Certs, sugar packs, a Swiss army knife, and a snakebite kit. The fourth compartment contains love notes, photos, postcards, perfume, sunglasses, nail polish, and plastic rain bonnets. The fifth compartment holds my wallet, which is a pocketbook in itself (don't get me started). Each compartment has its share of paper clips, bobby pins, pen caps, ticket stubs, rubber bands, earrings, and matches. Except for compartment number six, which is completely empty, just in case.

My beloved and I trudge through the parking lot and finally reach the mall of our dreams. Immediately Flash announces that she's famished, so we find a restaurant called Planet Lesbos. Our hostess, who wears nothing under her mesh T-shirt but two nipple rings, asks, "Table for two?"

I hold up three fingers. Flash looks at me. "Montana," I whisper, placing my bag on the chair to my left.

Flash shakes her head. "What do you have in there anyway?" she wonders out loud.

"Don't ask," I say, dumping the contents of our bread basket into compartment number six and motioning for Flash to pass the butter.

After we've eaten, we hit the mall. First stop, Sappho's Shoes. I dig Flash's heavy socks out of my bag and hand her a shoehorn too. Next we browse through my favorite bookstore, Read It and Weep, Sister. I dig around in my purse for Flash's reading glasses and buy a new unabridged edition of *Valley of the Dykes*. On our way to Dyke's Discount Drugs, Flash thinks she sees Raven across the way. I hand her a pair of binoculars so she can make sure.

"Is it Raven?" I ask.

"Yeah," she says, twisting the lenses to focus. "He's carrying a bag from Queer Gear, and he's got a piece of spinach in his teeth."

"Let me see." I fish a telescope out of my bag and get Raven into view.

"Oh, my God," Flash says, seeing what I'm up to. "What *don't* you have in that pocketbook?"

"Birth control pills," I answer, taking the binoculars back.

We march on. "Ooh, look at that dress," I say, pausing in front of Jodie's Closet, a very exclusive store that sells second-hand clothing direct from Hollywood.

"I'll wait out here," Flash says, seeing that I have already begun to drool.

I grab my wallet and ask Flash to hold Montana. Twenty minutes later I emerge with a bright red miniskirt. For some reason Flash's face is the same color as my purchase.

"Are you having a hot flash, Flash?" I ask my darling.

"No," she says. "I am dying of shame." She points to two jocks from her softball team who are laughing at the sight of their second basewoman carrying a pocketbook.

"Children can be so cruel," I say loudly, lifting my pocketbook off Flash's mortified shoulders. "Ready to go home?"

"Definitely. Give me the keys."

I reach into my bag and fumble through all six compartments. "Are you sure you gave them to me?" I ask.

"Of course I'm sure. Let me look."

"Nothing doing." The last woman who put her paws into Montana almost lost her arm at the elbow. It took the Jaws of Life to get her hand out. I rattle around my bag some more, but no luck. "I can't find them."

Flash sighs in exasperation. "Well, if you didn't have so much junk in there…"

"Junk? What junk? I don't have any junk in here. Unless you mean *this* piece of junk." I slap her wallet into her hand.

"And *this* piece of junk." I fling her checkbook at her. "And *this* piece of junk," I say, letting Flash's socks fly. "If you weren't cluttering up *my* bag with *your* junk, I'd be able to find the keys."

Flash looks at all the stuff in her hands. "And what would you like me to do with all this?"

"Carry it."

"Where?"

"In your pocket."

"And ruin the line of my jeans?"

"Well, if you would only carry a bag…"

"Fine," Flash says, walking off in a huff. I follow a few steps behind, until she stops in front of a store called Butch Bags. "You wait out here," she tells me, going inside. Ten minutes later Flash emerges and shows off her purchase. She's actually quite excited about it. "See," she says, "it's made of genuine imitation leather, and it has seven pockets: two on the inside, four on the outside, and a special little pocket for pens. Not only that, but it can also keep me warm in inclement weather. Ladies and gentlemen: The Butch Bag. Also known as The Jacket." Flash holds out her new jacket and twirls it around as if I am a bull about to charge. "I can wear it over my shoulder," she demonstrates, "or sling it across my arm or hold it in my hand. And best of all," Flash says, pausing for dramatic effect, "I got it for 30 percent off."

I have to admit, I'm totally impressed. "Flash," I say, "not only would my mother and my grandmother be proud of you, but I am proud of you."

My beloved beams as I reach into my pocketbook for a pair of scissors (kept in compartment number three). I snip off Flash's price tags and then hook my hand into the crook of her imitation leather-covered arm. "Ready to go?" I ask. She nods, and with that I exit the mall of my dreams with the butch of my dreams. And what more could any girl possibly want?

Hair Apparent

Flash comes home from work and finds me standing in front of the bathroom mirror with a paper bag over my head. Since Halloween is weeks away, this can mean only one thing.

"Having a bad hair day?" she asks.

"Yes," I mumble.

"Oh, good," says Flash.

Why does my hairdo disaster please my darling? Because, according to a recent survey, 97 percent of all American women worry about messing up their hair during sex. So if my hair already looks lousy, Flash figures she has a better chance of having her way with me. The statistic is rather frightening. What frightens me most about it is that only 3 percent of the female population have discovered the joy of being a femme top: I can do the do for hours and then climb off my beloved with every hair on my head still perfectly in place.

Flash cautiously lifts the paper bag off my head. "What's wrong with your hair?" she asks.

"It's flat."

"As opposed to round?"

"No, as opposed to full." I bend over from the waist, shake my head a few times, and then bounce back up. "See, like this." My hair retains a fluffy Julia Roberts morning-after-the-night-before look for 3.7 seconds before flattening out again. "I don't know." I study the mirror. "Flash, do you think I should cut my hair short?"

"If you want to."

"But do you think it would look good short?"

"Sure, it would look good short."

"So you don't think it looks good long?"

"I think it looks good long."

"So you don't think it would look good short?"

"I think it looks good right now."

"Oh, Flash," I say, sighing deeply. "You're only saying that because you love me. Let's say you didn't know me and you saw me walking down the street. Wouldn't you think my hair looked terrible?"

My beloved gives in. "All right. Your hair looks terrible."

"Flash!" I am devastated. "How can you say that?"

"I'm sorry. I didn't mean it. Your hair looks great."

"You call this great?" I frown at the mirror. "How can you say this looks great?"

"I give up." Flash heads for the kitchen and notices a bag on the table. "What's this?" she asks. "Chocolate mousse? Can I have some?"

"Don't eat that!" I yell. "That's for my hair."

Flash brings me the mousse. "Why don't you try a French braid?" she suggests. "Or a ponytail?"

"It's no use." I twist all my hair up into a bun and then let it fall loose again.

"C'mon, now," Flash says, trying to soothe me. "You're not having a bad hair day."

"You're right," I agree. "I'm having a bad hair *life*."

My hair has been nothing but trouble since the day I was born. Actually, my hair caused trouble in utero. I found this out when, upon doctor's orders, I asked my mother if she had taken DES when she was pregnant with me.

"No," she said. "I took T–U–M–S. Tums. *Oy*, did you give me heartburn. And you know what they say: Heartburn means a very hairy child. I was only afraid I shouldn't give birth to a little baby monkey."

Surprise, Ma. You gave birth to a little baby lesbian, who left the hospital three days later with her long black curly hair tied up in a pink ribbon — a femme from day one.

My curly hair and I got along fine through my wonder years. But then I turned thirteen. In 1968. Bad timing. Curly hair was out, and straight hair was in. We're talking surfer girls here. And my hair simply refused to go straight (just like the rest of me, though I didn't know that yet). First I tried the Tropicana trick. Since Anita Bryant didn't have a bad reputation yet, I thought nothing of rolling my hair around eight orange-juice cans every night. Of course, that meant I had to sleep sitting up, but who cared? As long as it worked. It didn't.

Next I tried the iron trick. I lay my head down on the ironing board like a chicken about to be slaughtered. My best friend stood over me, iron in one hand, spray starch in the other. But just as she was about to make contact, my mother walked in and gave such a scream, two cops came running.

"Who got murdered?" they asked.

"Nobody *yet*," my mother said, glaring at me. The phrase "If looks could kill" took on a whole new meaning from that point on.

I was determined to make my hair straight, as determined as my parents were, years later, to make me straight. I tried every goop, gel, spritz, and spray known to womankind. I Scotch-taped my bangs to my forehead. I used so many bobby pins, I set off metal detectors everywhere I went. I refused to leave the house on rainy days, which were guaranteed to make my hair frizz.

My parents, concerned about my growing obsession, took me to a shrink.

"Be your hair," Dr. Fraud said. "Speak in the voice of your hair. What does your hair want to say?"

I didn't hesitate. "I am not straight!" I shrieked at the top of my follicles. "I have never been straight. I will never be straight. Stop trying to make me straight!"

My parents, who were in the waiting room, rushed in, hysterical. I am probably the only person in the universe who has ever been outed by her own hair.

"Flash," I say, tearing myself away from the bathroom mirror and finding my better half in the living room. "Do you think I should call Buzz?"

"If you want to," Flash says, knowing better than to get involved.

I make the call, but of course Buzz, the most popular hairdresser in all of Lesbianville, can't see me for two whole weeks.

I count the hours as though he were my long-lost lover. I read dozens of fashion magazines and cut out pictures of movie stars with hair to die for. My own crowning glory looks worse and worse as the days go by. *Rat's nest,* I think. *Weed patch. Mop.*

Finally the hour arrives. I wash, condition, and blow-dry my hair, since of course I only let Buzz see me at my best. Five minutes before my appointment, I rush to the mirror to check my hair one last time. All of a sudden my hair looks gorgeous. Stunning. Absolutely perfect. I grab the phone and tell Buzz I have a migraine. He is all sympathy. Twenty minutes later I catch sight of myself in the mirror again. I look awful. I call back.

"Miraculous recovery?" Buzz asks. We've been down this road before.

I arrive at Buzz Cuts and let Buzz lead me to his chair. He drapes a lavender smock around my neck. "What are we doing today?" he asks, running his fingers lightly through my hair.

Instantly I look fabulous. There's nothing like being fussed over by a beauty queen. "How did you do that?" I ask. "Won't you please move in with me and Flash?" I beg him, not for the first time. I tell him I want all my hair cut off.

"No, no, no." Buzz is adamant. "The Sinéad O'Connor look is definitely out this year." He thinks for a minute. "What about the Margarethe Cammermeyer look?"

"Too butch."

"You're right." He plays with my hair a little. "How about a Madonna look?"

"Which one?"

"Her Breathless Mahoney phase."

"Perfect."

Buzz agrees and starts to snip. Soon the floor is covered with dark wet curls, and my hair is up to my shoulders. I stare into the mirror, dubious.

"Don't get hysterical. It's longer than it looks," Buzz assures me.

"Sure," I pout. "I bet you say that to all the boys."

"Don't be vicious," he says, snipping dangerously close to my ear.

Buzz blow-dries my hair, and I have to admit it does look good. I also know better than to expect that I'll be able to get my hair to do this at home. I say as much to Buzz, and he clucks in understanding. "It's hard to blow yourself and get good results," he sympathizes. "Believe me, I've tried."

Buzz reminds me that my hair is in shock. So is my girl-friend. When she gets home that night, she blinks in surprise. "I thought you were just getting a trim," she says, reaching out to feel my hair.

"Don't touch it!" I yell, slapping away her hand. "You'll flatten it."

"I can't pet your hair anymore?" Flash asks.

"No petting," I say. "You can squeeze, you can scrunch, you can fluff, but you can't pet. So what do you think?" I pirouette slowly so Flash can check out every angle. "Do you like it?" I ask.

"It's cute," she says, but her voice betrays her.

"You don't like it," I say.

"I have to get used to it," she reminds me.

"I knew you wouldn't like my hair short."

"I like your hair short."

"So you didn't like my hair long?"

"No, I liked your hair long."

"So you don't like my hair short?"

"I like it short. I think it looks fine."

"But you wish it was long."

"I don't wish it was long. I'm happy that it's short."

"Too bad, because I'm growing it out again."

"Maybe I should grow my hair long," Flash says, running her fingers through her DA.

"No!" I look at Flash in horror. "I love your hair."

"Well, I love your hair. You know why?"

"Why?"

"Because it belongs to you."

"Oh, Flash." I leap on top of my girlfriend and, in a burst of love, let her mess up my hair as much as she likes.

And that's the long and short of it.

Butch in Training

"Package for you." Flash huffs and puffs and deposits an enormous carton onto the kitchen table with a groan.

"Who's it from?"

"Your editor."

"My editor? What could she be sending me?"

I watch curiously as Flash slices the box open with her pocketknife and dumps the contents onto the table. Envelopes, envelopes everywhere, as far as the eye can see.

"Fan mail!" I shriek, tossing a fistful into the air. I grab one as it falls from the sky and open it with glee. But there's no letter inside. Just a photo. And not just any photo. It's a portrait of a femme wearing nothing but butt floss.

"What is this?" I pick up the envelope for a clue and notice it's addressed to my beloved. "Flash, this is for you."

"Let me see it."

"Not on your life."

"Hey, this one's for me too." Flash opens an envelope that smells like Poison clear across the room. " 'Dear Flash,' " she reads out loud. " 'I am a 22-year-old blonde buxom blue-eyed femme, looking for a butch…' "

"Give me that." I snatch the letter away as Flash opens another.

" 'Dear Flash, if you ever come to your senses and leave that woman…' "

"Are they all for you?" I can't help but whine.

"No." Flash fishes an envelope from the pile. "This one's addressed to Raven."

"Oh, for God's sake." I continue the search and finally find an envelope with my name on it. " 'Dear Lesléa,' " I read. " 'I've been reading your column for years, and I've just got to know: Is Flash really as wonderful as you make her out to be? If so, do you share?' "

Now, listen up, ladies: Of course Flash is not as wonderful as I make her out to be. She is a thousand times more wonderful than mere words on paper could possibly convey. And no, I do not share. Even as a child I never let anyone near my favorite toy, so get over it, girlfriend.

But I will let you in on a little secret: When I first met Flash, she was a tiny bit rough around the edges. I wasn't worried, though. Most butches can and need to be trained. You too can turn your butch into a dream butch and have her eating out of your hand (or any other body part you desire) in the wink of a false eyelash. But you must begin immediately.

Unbeknownst to Flash, I started training her on our very first date. I have to give her credit: She knew enough to ask me out for Saturday night, and she knew enough to pick me up at 8:00. (If your butch says, "Let's get together Tuesday night. Do you want to drive, or should I?" forget it.) Flash knew enough to arrive in a freshly pressed shirt, creased pants, and snappy shoes, and she knew enough not to be late.

Flash even knew enough to bring me a flower. A rose, in fact. Which I'm sure would have pleased the average femme. But I am not the average femme. I am what some call a high femme. I prefer to be known as a high-maintenance femme. While Flash meant well, it was clear to me she needed to learn some basic math: Diamonds come one by one. Shoes come in pairs. Roses come by the dozen.

Since butches tend to be so sensitive, I approached the subject with my usual tact. I took the rose and said "Thank you" like a lady. Then I got out a huge vase and ran enough water in it to fill the Atlantic.

"Don't you have anything smaller?" Flash asked.

"No," I said, setting the lonely rose on the table, making a visual point.

A minute later Flash made mistake number two. "You look nice," she said. The average femme would have taken that to be a compliment. But this high-maintenance femme hadn't spent the last two weeks shopping for the perfect outfit and the last seven hours bathing, shaving, bleaching, filing, polishing, combing, brushing, drying, moussing, spritzing, spraying, and applying five pounds of makeup to have all her efforts summed up in one little four-letter word. I started at the bottom and worked my way up.

"Do you like these shoes?" I asked Flash, pirouetting on my three-inch heels.

"They're fabulous," she answered.

"And do you think I look okay in such a short skirt?" I ran my hands along·the fabric.

"You look really good in it."

"What about my perfume — is it too sweet?" I waved my wrist in front of her nose.

"You smell wonderful."

"Do you think my hair looks good like this?" I fussed in front of the mirror.

"Your hair looks great."

When I felt sufficiently admired, I announced that I was ready to go and glanced at my wrap, which was draped over a chair. Flash didn't move, so I picked up my coat, handed it to her, and turned around. Then I backed up and slid my arms into the sleeves. "Thanks," I said with a sweet smile.

When we got down to her car, Flash made another faux pas by walking around to the driver's side and starting to get in. I stood on the sidewalk by the passenger door, waiting. When she yelled, "It's open," I yelled back, "It doesn't look open to me."

Soon we were both in the car, heading for a cozy little restaurant on the outskirts of Lesbianville. After Flash parked the car and got out, I watched her walk halfway across the parking lot before she realized that she was alone and that unless she wanted to eat her dinner that way, she had better turn around, come back, and open the car door for me. I took her arm as if it already belonged to me (the better to steer you with, my dear) and maneuvered her across the pavement, letting go just as she opened the restaurant's door so I could enter first.

Once at our table I decided to simply sit down rather than instruct Flash on the fine art of pulling out a lady's chair for her. I saved that lesson for our second date so as not to overwhelm her. However, when our waiter asked us what we wanted to drink and Flash said without hesitation "I'll have a..." I simply had to knock my knife clear across the room and ask her to retrieve it so I could order my glass of white wine before she asked for her Budweiser.

During dinner I taught Flash how to pay complete attention to a femme. When she started concentrating on something else — like her food, for example — I shrugged my shoulder just so, causing the spaghetti strap of my bustier to slide down my arm in a slow, mesmerizing manner.

At dessert time I ordered chocolate mousse and used my tongue to maximum effect. Assuming that Flash, like most butches, was completely fascinated — and baffled — by all my feminine accoutrements, I searched through my purse frequently. (*What in the world does she have in there?* I could practically hear Flash wondering.) I touched up my lipstick at the table, of course. (*How does she do that without a mirror?* Flash silently marveled.) Before the meal was through, I had done my job and convinced her that I was, without a doubt, the femme of her dreams and the woman she could simply not live without.

When Flash took me home at the end of the evening, I could tell she was nervous. She pulled into my driveway and kept the motor running. I gave her an insulted look that said, *Don't you think I'm attractive enough to see the evening through?* Immediately she shut off the engine, which prompted another indignant look: *How dare you presume I want you to come in?* The poor girl didn't know whether she was coming or going, which is just the way I wanted her.

"May I have the honor of coming inside?" Flash finally asked and in fact still asks every time we come home from a date, even though we've been living together for over six years.

Once inside I set the mood with candles, music, and wine. I motioned for Flash to sit down on the couch, and then I sat on her lap, closed my eyes, and puckered my lips. When she finally kissed me, I acted surprised, as if it were all her idea. Then I let her take the lead, and she proved to be my dream butch by making all my dreams come true.

But who knew I was creating a monster? Here we are, years later, with Flash up to her elbows in fan mail from femmes fatales, and I don't like it one bit.

"Listen to this one," Flash says. " 'Dear Flash, I am writing a book called *Butches Are From Mars, Femmes Are From Venus,* and I have a feeling you would be the perfect research assistant...' "

"Dream on, sister," I say, plucking the letter out of Flash's hand. "You are not to answer any of these letters," I tell her in a stern voice. "I'll answer them."

"Don't tell me you're jealous," Flash says.

"Jealous? I'm not jealous," I say, picking up a pen. "I'm just going to thank all your fans for writing and let them know that if they even think about sending any more letters…"

"Watch what you write," Flash says nervously. "I don't want them all to think I'm henpecked."

"You're not henpecked, Flash," I tell her.

"I'm not?" She sounds surprised.

"Of course not," I remind her. "You're pussy-whipped."

"Pussy-whipped? I'll show you who's pussy-whipped."

Flash shoves all the envelopes to the floor, picks me up, and slings me over her shoulder like a mail sack. She carries me off to the bedroom, where she proves yet again just who wears the pants in this family. And if she wants to think that was all her idea, who am I not to let her?

Have Femme, Will Travel

"Tell me I'm dreaming," Flash moans. "Tell me this is a nightmare."

"This is a nightmare," I tell Flash. "But you're not dreaming." I shake my head at the sorry sight before my eyes: my beloved Flash sitting in her beloved car, the back tires on solid ground, the front wheels up to their hubcaps in sand.

How did this happen? This was not part of our vacation plan. The plan was to enjoy two long, luxurious, stress-free weeks on Cape Cod. Tonight we were supposed to drive into Provincetown for a show featuring the world-famous drag queen Lotta Sequins.

I'd gotten all dressed up (not to be outdone by the boys) in my shortest skirt, longest earrings, highest heels, and biggest hair. Flash, looking dapper in her black silk shirt and chinos, steered into the parking lot and started searching for a space. The place was jammed, so she headed for the back of the lot, never dreaming that trouble lurked just around the corner in the form of a sand trap disguised as the last available parking space on the planet. Who could even imagine that the Goddess would be so cruel?

"Maybe you should get out of the car, Flash," I gently suggest. "We'll see the show and deal with this later."

"Are you crazy?" Flash argues, remaining behind the steering wheel, a true captain ready to go down with her ship.

All of a sudden I realize who I am dealing with here: a butch. In other words, a woman who appreciates a good truck as much as a good fuck. A woman who won't pick up a dust rag inside the house but spends hours every weekend washing, waxing, buffing, polishing, and vacuuming her car (not to mention cleaning out the stick shift grooves with a toothpick).

Flash has actually said that if she were going to be marooned on a desert island and could take only one thing with her (besides me, of course), she would take her car. I, on the other hand, would take my pocketbook, which is big enough to hold Flash, Flash's car, and anything else I might possibly need, but that's another story. To me, a car is a hunk of metal someone else drives me around in. To Flash, a car is a thing of beauty and a joy forever.

Maybe this is hard for me to understand because I grew up in Brooklyn, where nobody owns a car. That's because there's nowhere to put it, unless you have enough money to pay for a garage space, which costs more than your rent, and if you had that kind of money, why in the world would you live in Brooklyn?

When my family moved to Long Island, I spent years looking for the subway stops. It finally dawned on me that there weren't any because everyone's house came with a two-car garage. Which meant they had cars and all knew how to drive. Which meant I had to learn how to drive too.

I signed up for driver's ed the day I turned seventeen. My teacher, Miss Ford, spent the entire first lesson teaching me how to get in and out of the car like a lady. For those of you who missed this important lesson, pay attention: First you gently lower your derriere onto the seat, keeping your back straight and your head high. Then, with your knees pressed tightly together, your thighs parallel to the ground, and your knees bent at a perfect ninety-degree angle, you use your stomach muscles to slowly lift your legs and *swivel* your gams into the car. I had to practice this maneuver for weeks, both on the driver's side (swiveling left to right) and the passenger side (swiveling right to left) before Miss Ford would actually let me take the car out on the road.

Then came the big day: my driver's test. Actually, it was a series of big days, since I had to take my road test five times. It wasn't my fault, though. The officer, Mr. Steel (named for his nerves), truly had it in for me. He asked me to parallel park on a hill. He told me to change lanes just as we were approaching a traffic light (of course I didn't see it was red; I was too busy looking in my rearview mirror). Mr. Steel made me so nervous, my three-point turn turned into a 23-point turn.

"We've got to stop meeting like this," I said to him as I got into the car for my fourth try. He didn't crack a smile but immediately flunked me for sticking the key into the ignition *before* I fastened my seat belt, even though I hadn't even turned the car on yet.

That did it. Clearly, drastic measures were needed. On the day of my fifth road test, I wore the shortest miniskirt my mother would let me out of the house in and proceeded to get into the car exactly the way a lady shouldn't. Needless to say, Mr. Steel passed me with flying colors.

And I'm proud to say that I have never been in an accident or even had major car trouble since (of course, I only drive to the shoe store and back). Oh, except for that time when I drove from Lesbianville to New York and my muffler fell off on the way home. I did what any quick-thinking femme would do: I wiggled out of my panty hose, tied the muffler back on with them, and drove home without a hitch.

"You did what?" Flash asked, aghast. "Do you know how dangerous that is?"

The next day she came home loaded down with maps, matches, jumper cables, jacks, flares, flashlights, gas cans, blankets, freeze-dried dinner packets, and a huge banner that says HELP! Which is what I needed to fit it all into my car. "And I got you this too," Flash said, handing me a small gift box, exquisitely wrapped.

"What's this?" I gasped, tearing at the ribbon. Inside was a plastic card. "A charge card!" I squealed.

"Not exactly. It's a Triple A card. Do not," Flash said sternly, "ever leave home without it."

"Where's yours?" I asked.

"I don't need one," Flash boasted. Sure, she can change her oil, change a tire, jump-start the ignition, and jimmy a lock, but clearly she cannot tow her car. Luckily, she always has her femme in tow, and luckier still, her femme always follows her butch's advice. I'll have our car out of this sand trap in no time.

I dig my Triple A card out of my pocketbook and flash it at Flash. "I'll be right back. Don't go anywhere," I say, trying to make her laugh. Her face is as uncrackable as Mr. Steel's.

I make my way through the parking lot into the theater. Before I have a chance to look around the lobby for a pay phone, I am bombarded by a middle-aged couple. Both husband and wife are decked out in matching outfits: Hawaiian-print Bermuda shorts and T-shirts emblazoned with MY SON CAME OUT AND ALL I GOT WAS THIS LOUSY T-SHIRT.

"Ooh, look, George. He looks just like a woman."

"You're wrong, Ethel. See his feet? They're *huge*. They say you can always tell by the feet."

I look around and then realize to my horror that George and Ethel are talking about *me*. "I *am* a woman," I bark at them, "*not* a drag queen."

"Oh, it's definitely a man," George decides. "The voice is a dead giveaway."

"I am *not* a man!" I shout now, stomping my gigantic foot on the ground.

"He really believes he's a woman," George marvels.

"*She,* George, you're supposed to call them *she.* Take a picture, take a picture."

Ethel puts her arm around my waist and smiles as George snaps away. Someone else asks for my autograph. In a moment of divine inspiration, I come up with my drag name: Dusty Tchotchkes. A crowd gathers. "You'll all have to excuse me," I apologize. "It's almost show time." And with those words I make a dash backstage into Lotta Sequins's dressing room.

"Darling, you look *fabulous.*" Lotta kisses me on the cheek. "Oh, that skirt, those earrings. Those *shoes.* I've just got to try them on." I kick off my shoes, and Lotta slides her size-25 feet into them. They fit perfectly.

"Listen, Lotta," I say. "I'll trade you those pumps for the use of your phone."

"Oh, my God," Lotta shrieks, "you're a girl!" At least Lotta knows a real female voice when she hears one. She puts her hands on her hips and glares. "What the hell is this, *Victor/Victoria?*"

I explain the situation, and Lotta could not have been more gracious. She shows me to the phone, where I spend fifteen minutes listening to Muzak before I get someone on the wire. "They'll be there within the hour," the dispatcher tells me.

I race outside to tell Flash. The girl is up and out of her car, directing traffic. "You, in the white Toyota, back that baby up. This aisle has to stay clear. A tow truck's coming through." I watch my butch with pride. All those years working traffic control at the Michigan Womyn's Music Festival had definitely paid off.

"Hey, where are your shoes?" Flash says, looking at my bare feet.

"Don't ask." I shake my head. "Listen, I've got good news. Triple A will be here in an hour."

Yeah, right. And I'm Barbra Streisand. After exactly fifty-nine minutes have passed, I go back into the theater to call again.

"Oh, you're in Provincetown?" the dispatcher says. "I thought you said Providence."

"Providence? You mean Rhode Island?" I try to keep my voice down, since Lotta Sequins is onstage doing a soft Bette Midler number.

The dispatcher assures me she'll send someone right away, and I hurry outside to inform Flash. Just as Lotta starts belting out "Enough Is Enough," the tow truck arrives.

"Hi, I'm Diesel." A woman with short black hair climbs out of the truck and shakes Flash's hand. I don't know why I'm surprised to see a dyke. I mean, this is Provincetown, after all.

Diesel looks as if she could lift Flash's car out of the sand with her bare hands. She gets out the chains, drags them over to our helpless vehicle, and disappears underneath the car to assess the situation. Without saying a word to us, she gets up, goes back into the tow truck, revs the engine, and roars away.

"My car!" Flash screams, envisioning her pride and joy jolted out of the sand and flying through the air like a cartoon.

"Relax, Flash, she didn't hook the chains on yet." I try to soothe my beloved, whose gay nerves are clearly shot.

Diesel comes back. "I needed more of a lead," she explains, squatting down again. This time she attaches the chains to the car and then walks back to the tow truck to turn on the juice.

Flash kneels to the ground. "C'mon, baby. C'mon, baby. You can do it, baby. That's it, that's it. Do it for me, baby. Yes, yes, yes," she croons as if she's egging me on to orgasm rather than coaxing her car out of the sand.

Finally the car begins to move. A minute later all four wheels are on solid ground. And two minutes after that, Flash is back behind the wheel, and we head out of the parking lot, with Lotta Sequins's encore, "Everything's Coming Up Roses," ringing in our ears.

"God, that was a drag," Flash says.

"You don't know the half of it." I tell Flash all about George, Ethel, and Dusty Tchotchkes.

She smiles for the first time all night. "Thank God they didn't ask you to sing," she says.

"R-E-S-P-E-C-T," I remind Flash, imitating a young, gifted, and tone-deaf Aretha.

"Please," Flash begs. "Tell you what. If you stop singing, I'll buy you a new pair of shoes tomorrow."

That shuts me up fast. I zip my lips and remain silent all the way home, glad that the evening didn't turn out to be a total loss after all.

The Pen Is Mightier Than the Charge Card

It's that time of the month again. I sit in front of the television, weeping at the sight of that Michelin baby up to his double chin in tires; Murphy Brown tossing her little son, Avery, up in the air like a Frisbee; Roseanne and Jackie fighting about whether dressing Jackie's son in pink will make him likely to be a little light in his loafers. Even the sight of little Ricky, who must be at least my age by now, crawling through an old *I Love Lucy* rerun, brings tears to my eyes.

"Hey, Flash," I call, but my beloved is nowhere in sight. This is not an issue she cares to discuss. But she can't avoid me forever. I crawl into bed and pretend to be asleep. As soon as she slips in beside me, I whip off my leopard-print beauty mask and whine, "But our baby would be so cute, Flash. She would have my hair, your eyes…"

"Have you forgotten that two dykes cannot a baby make?" Flash always was a stickler for details. She studies my pout for a minute and then comes up with an idea. "Hey, I know how to cheer you up. I'll take you on a field trip tomorrow."

"Where?"

"It's a surprise."

"But how will I know what to wear?"

"Dress casual," she says. "Now go to sleep."

The next morning I am up bright and early, all ready to go in a short black dress and low suede heels.

"I said *casual*," Flash reminds me, giving my outfit the once-over.

"This *is* casual," I remind her. "If I were getting dressed up, I'd be wearing longer earrings, higher heels, shinier bracelets, darker lipstick..."

"Okay, you're right. Let's just go."

We get into the car, and Flash drives to the outskirts of Lesbianville. Soon we pull into the parking lot of a store called the Joy of Toys.

"Oh, Flash, you devil, you." I break my own rule and leap out of the car before she even has a chance to open my door for me. I have been trying to get my beloved ex-nun to come to a sex shop with me for *years*.

I race into the store and immediately see, to my great disappointment, that we're not talking sex toys here. We're talking toy toys. And mothering gadgets. Instead of tit clamps, I see breast pumps. Rubber pants instead of edible underwear. Mickey Mouse sheets versus black satin sheets. Books with titles like *Ten Tricks to Keep Your Child in Bed All Night* instead of *Ten Tricks to Keep Your Lover in Bed All Night*. Is this really what I want my life to look like?

Oh, but the babies. They're everywhere: Twelve babies screaming, eleven babies shouting, ten babies crying, nine babies drooling, eight babies burping, seven babies belching, six babies pooping. Five sets of twins! Four grabbing babies, three kicking babies, two spitting babies, and one baby barfing on my shoe.

I give *my* baby a look that says, *Get me out of here!* and we hustle out to the car double-time. "Thanks a lot, Flash," I say, glaring at her and rubbing my heel with a Kleenex. "These shoes are *ruined.*"

"Just a little dose of reality, dear," my beloved says, steering the car toward home.

I suppose Flash is right. The point isn't whether I want a baby or not. The point is that I'd make a lousy mother. Which reminds me for the millionth time, I don't really want to *be* a mommy — I want to *have* a mommy.

"Flash," I say, "do you realize my mother hasn't called me in six months?"

"Your dialing finger wasn't broken last time I looked."

"You're right," I say. "I'm a lousy daughter."

"It's never too late to have a happy childhood," Flash says, reading the bumper sticker on the Subaru in front of us. I take that as a sign to mend my relationship with my mother. I decide to call her once a week, like a good daughter should.

Sunday afternoon rolls around, and I still haven't managed to pick up the receiver. Finally Flash points to the phone at 4:59. We both know there's no way I'm going to call after 5:00 once the rates go up. I shoo Flash out of my room, sit down on the couch, and dial.

"Hello?"

"Hi, Ma."

"I think you have the wrong number." She hangs up.

I call back. "Ma, it's me."

"Hello? Who is this?"

"It's me."

"Who?"

"Your daughter."

"Oh, it's *you.* I didn't recognize your voice." (Translation: My own child hasn't called me in so long, I've forgotten what my own flesh and blood sounds like.) "So what's new?"

"Um…" I rack my brain. Why is it that I have nothing to say to my mother after not talking to her for six months? I talk to Raven about fifteen times a day, and I always have at least twenty-five new things to tell him each time I call. Think, think, think. "Well, Flash and I went away to Maine last weekend."

"Really? How was the weather?"

The weather? My darling and I never emerged from the depths of our hotel room long enough to find out, which was the whole point of getting away. "It was okay, I guess."

"It didn't rain? Here it was very wet all weekend."

There it was very wet all weekend too, but I doubt my mother wants to hear about *that*. I try to change the subject. "Ma, I'm going on a book tour for my new anthology of lesbi — "

"Rain, rain, rain, from Friday night to Sunday afternoon," she interrupts. "It was coming down in buckets, I'm telling you."

"Lesbian love poems," I say, finishing my sentence. "They're sending me to New York, D.C., Chicago, Denver, San Francisco, L.A.…"

"It's very cold in Chicago — you know they have that wind there that comes off the lake. And Denver — I think they have snow there already. L.A. is nice, if they don't have an earthquake. San Francisco is damp, you'll need a sweater…"

I try to change the subject again. "What did you do this weekend?"

"Oh, it was such a nice weekend. Saturday it was warm, but not too hot. It got cloudy in the afternoon, but it didn't rain. It threatened to rain, and maybe there was a drop or two, but it wasn't a big deal, nothing to talk about really…"

Then why are you talking about it? I want to scream. But of course I don't. My beloved sticks her head inside my room, and suddenly I get an idea. "Listen, Ma, I gotta go. They're talking about Flash floods."

"Really? Those can be very dangerous."

"I know. I'll call you." I hang up the phone. And sit there. And sit there. And sit there. All of a sudden I feel like I may never be able to get off this couch again.

Flash, smelling trouble, comes in and sits beside me. "Hey, it was only the first call. Maybe things will go better when you call next week."

"Why would I call next week?"

"Because you said you were going to call your mother every week."

I look at my beloved like she's lost her mind. "I never said that, Flash. You must be hearing things."

My darling ignores me. "Anyway, you have to call her next week," she says. "Next Sunday is your mother's birthday."

"What should I get her?" I think for a minute. "I know. What about those storm-chaser videos from the Weather Channel?"

Flash ignores me again. "I think," she says, "you should write a poem for your mother."

"Oh, no." I say. "That's not fair." Flash knows I can't refuse a writing assignment. I pick up a pen and begin:

Everything I Need to Know About Life, I Learned From My Mother

If the shoe fits, buy three pairs (in black, brown, and navy).

Talk is cheap (especially after 11:00 and on weekends).

There's no such thing as a fat-free lunch.

Beauty is in the eye of the beautician.

If you don't have anything to say, keep talking.

A leopard-print skirt can never change its spots.

Just say no to retail.

Who cares if the glass is half full or half empty, as long as it's from Tiffany's?

I show my masterpiece to Flash, who isn't quite sure how it will be received. "Trust me, she'll love it," I say, putting the poem in the mail.

The following Sunday the phone rings. "Hello?"

"Is this my daughter the writer?"

I must be dreaming. I've waited ten years and twenty books to hear those words. "Ma, is that you?"

"Of course it's me. I love the poem."

"You do?"

"Of course I do. It's hanging on the refrigerator." This is the ultimate compliment. I can just picture the poem anchored in its place of honor with magnets that look like miniature Oreo cookies and hot fudge sundaes. "Why didn't you ever tell me you were such a good writer?"

"You never asked."

"So I'm asking. What are you working on now?"

Gulp. I'm working on a play. Act One begins at the Clit Club, where a punk dyke wearing a PUSSY: BREAKFAST OF CHAMPIONS T-shirt is telling the bouncer about falling in love with the lady who pierced her labia. I can't possibly tell my mother that. "Um, how's the weather there?" I ask her. "Here it's unseasonably warm — hot, really. In fact, I'm *shvitzing* from just holding the receiver against my ear…"

"You must be working on something interesting," my mother says.

"In fact, there's some heat lightning going on, and I think I heard thunder a minute ago. Well, maybe it wasn't thunder, maybe it was our next-door neighbor shutting her garage door, but still, just to be on the safe side, we'd better get off the phone."

You know what they say: Like mother, like daughter.

Nun of the Above

Here's a pop quiz for all you gay history buffs: What extraordinary, earth-shattering event occurred on August 5, 1962?

A) Marilyn Monroe died

B) Flash entered the convent

C) All of the above

As I'm sure you all know, the correct answer is C. Now, for 200 bonus points, which of the following statements is true:

A) Marilyn Monroe, upon hearing that Flash was no longer available, did herself in (as I've said a million times, a good butch is hard to find).

B) Flash, after crossing M.M.'s name off her list of potential girlfriends, decided to take a vow of chastity (after all, a good femme is also hard to find, and I was only seven at the time).

C) Sister Flash ain't telling.

Every year, around the beginning of August, my beloved grows nostalgic for the nunnery. She dons her SISTERS ARE DOING IT FOR THEMSELVES T-shirt, which depicts two nubile nuns in a compromising position, and plays Casselberry-

DuPreé's "Did Jesus Have a Baby Sister?" over and over on the stereo. Then she brings out the photo albums and gives me a tour of the past. "There's Mother Masochist," Flash says, pointing to a grim-looking woman.

"Why does she look so pained?"

"She's kneeling on a cheese grater."

"I see. And who's this with the whip?" I point to another nun.

"That's Sister Sadist. The two of them were always together."

"I thought you weren't allowed to have 'particular friendships,' " I say. I know the lingo. "Did you have a particular friendship, Flash?"

"Um...not really."

"Flash." I give her a stern look. "Isn't it a sin to lie to your wife?"

"It's a sin for me to *have* a wife," Flash reminds me as she quickly turns a few pages.

I grab the album and flip back the pages she's skipped until I come to a young nun who's hiking up her habit to reveal a shapely thigh. "Who's this? Sister Sexpot?"

"Oh, *her.*" Flash gets a faraway look in her eye. "That's Sister Lola Brigid. Uh, I guess you could say we had a few good times together."

"Say no more."

Flash has already confessed to me all about Sister Lola Brigid. The two naughty nuns managed to keep their affair under their habits for a few years before Mother Superior caught on and told Flash, "You must choose between Lola and the Lord." Flash chose Lola, but Lola chose a husband and fourteen children (once a Catholic, always a Catholic).

I think Flash and I should celebrate the day she left the convent, Lola or no Lola, not the day she went in. After all, if she hadn't left, Flash would still be married to that other Jewish martyr as opposed to this one. But Flash insists, so every year we mark the day: One year we saw *Nunsense,* the next year we saw *Sister Act.* One year we rented *The Singing Nun,* the next year we rented *The Flying Nun.* Last year we got drunk on a bottle of Blue Nun and played an X-rated version of Mother Superior, May I? all night. I don't know what we're going to do this year, but no need to worry: Flash has the answer.

"Look what came in the mail today." My beloved waves an envelope with excitement. "An invitation to Sister Mike's golden anniversary."

"Who's Sister Mike?"

"She was in charge of all the young nuns when I first went into the convent. I can't believe she's been a nun for fifty years."

"Wow." That is impressive. I mean, to stay married to anyone for fifty years in this day and age, let alone Jesus Christ, is certainly an accomplishment. I take the invitation from Flash and study it. "How come this says Sister Mary Maria Marie?"

"That's her official name," Flash says, "but to us nuns, she was always Sister Mike. I can't wait to see her."

"You mean, we're going?"

"I wouldn't miss it," Flash says. "The Sisters of Perpetual Latency are *known* for their parties. And besides, it's on August 5th, and you know what that means."

"What?"

Flash folds her hands, and an angelic look appears on her face. "God works in mysterious ways," she says, proving that you can take the nun out of the convent but you can't take the convent out of the ex-nun.

August 5th dawns bright and sunny. I dress for the occasion in a black miniskirt, Madonna T-shirt, and crucifix earrings.

"You are not leaving the house like that," Flash says, sounding like my mother. I reluctantly change into a modest knee-length skirt and proper white blouse. Flash approves, so off we go in her car, and before I can sing "Like a Prayer" for the twenty-third time, we arrive at Flash's alma mater.

"Let's go in the main entrance," Flash says, pulling open the door. We enter a great hall, which appears deserted. "Maybe we should try the side door," Flash says.

Just as we turn to go, a voice booms out of nowhere, "You're late, Sister Flash." My beloved starts shaking like the Cowardly Lion in that scene where Dorothy and company meet the Wizard of Oz. I've never seen my butch so frightened before.

"Relax, Flash," I say, trying to soothe her. "What do you think that was, the voice of God?"

"No, much w-w-worse," she stammers. "That was M-M-Mother G-G-General."

Mother General? Should I salute? Before I can ask, the Grand Pooh-Bah of Mothers comes out from behind a curtain. Mother General is at least eight feet tall and just as wide. Seeing that her mere presence has reduced my big, brave butch to a mass of quivering Jell-O, I step forward. "Hello, Mother General," I say, extending my hand. "I'm — "

"Silence!" Mother General thunders, causing me to run shrieking back to Flash. "The Great and Powerful Mother General knows who you are and why you have come. And I have every intention of granting your wish to see Sister Mary Maria Marie."

"Oh, th-th-thank you, M-M-Mother G-G-General." Flash falls trembling to her knees.

"Silence!" Mother General barks again. "Now off with you to the social hall before I change my mind."

"C'mon." I pull Flash to her feet and keep hold of her hand as we make a break for it, in case she decides to do a swan dive through a stained glass window or something.

Finally we arrive at the social hall, where Sister Mike's party is in full swing. Nuns are drinking punch, priests are eating hosts, and a choir of altar boys — whose members bear a striking resemblance to Lesbianville's Gay Men's Chorus — are singing "I Will Follow Him."

"Where's Sister Mike?" I ask Flash, but before she can answer, a flock of five nuns swarms around us.

"Hello, Sister Flash!" they greet my beloved in unison. Flash introduces me to Sister Dolly, Sister Holly, Sister Lolly, Sister Molly, and Sister Polly.

"Charmed."

"Delighted."

"Pleased to meet you."

"Enchanté."

"The pleasure is all yours."

"Aren't they something?" Flash chuckles. "They're sisters."

"I know they're sisters," I scold Flash. "Why else would they be wearing habits?"

"No, I mean they're *sisters,*" Flash says.

"Not brothers."

"Not cousins."

"Not friends."

"Not foes."

"Not lovers." Sister Polly gives Flash a pointed look.

"We better go find Sister Mike," Flash says, leading me toward the guest of honor.

"Sister Flash! I knew you'd come." Sister Mike has that deep, gravelly Harvey Fierstein kind of voice that makes this femme weak in the knees. She looks me up and down and then turns back to Flash. "Who's this, your roommate?"

"No, Sister Mike," Flash says. "She's my companion."

"Your companion? Sister Flash, shame on you." Flash hangs her head. Sister Mike lets a long moment pass before she growls, "I believe the correct, respectful term is *beloved* companion."

Flash lifts her head. "You mean you approve?" she dares to ask.

"Of course I approve." She gives Flash a slap on the back that sends my poor beloved companion flying. "Congratulations. She's a hell of a lot cuter than Sister Lola Brigid."

"Is she here?" I ask, eager to get a look at the competition.

"No, my child." Sister Mike rolls her eyes. "She couldn't get a baby-sitter."

"Too bad," Flash says.

Sister Mike and I both throw her a dirty look.

"I sure am thirsty, Sister Flash," Sister Mike rasps. "Why don't you go get us some refreshments?"

Flash hurries off, and Sister Mike motions for me to sit beside her. "Can I ask you a personal question?" she says, leaning forward.

"Sure." I lean forward too.

"What do you think of these shoes?" Sister Mike lifts the hem of her habit very discreetly.

"Oh, they're very nice, Sister Mike. Chunky heels are in this year."

"You don't think they're too..." she pauses, lowering her husky voice even further, "femmey?"

"Oh, no, Sister. On someone else, maybe, but you can definitely get away with it."

Satisfied, Sister Mike drops her skirt just as Flash returns with punch, Pope-sicles, and sandwiches.

"Isn't the food heavenly?" Sister Mike asks.

"The rolls are out of this world," I answer.

"Nun buns," Sister Mike says. "Here, take some for the road." She motions for me to open my pocketbook and dumps in a dozen.

"We'd better be off," Flash says, helping me to my feet.

"You can't leave now," Sister Mike says. "The band hasn't played yet."

"There's a band?"

"Mary and the Magdalenes. Look, they're just about to start." And sure enough, the singing nuns break into their first number: a slow but steady rendition of "Song of the Soul."

"Flash," I whisper. "This song is practically the Lesbian National Anthem."

Flash shrugs "Go figure."

"I believe Cris Williamson sings it," Sister Mike adds in her scratchy voice.

Then, as if on cue, all the nuns stand and form a circle. Soon we are all singing the chorus, swaying back and forth with our arms linked behind us. And as I stand there between Flash and Sister Mike, I can't help asking myself the following questions:

A) Am I still at the convent, or have I been beamed up to the Michigan Womyn's Music Festival?

B) Did Flash just goose me on the behind, or was that a love pinch from Sister Mike?

C) Is that a nun bun in Mother General's pocket, or is she just happy to see me?

Of course, the correct answer to all three questions is "I don't know." Which is fine with me. Because a sister is a sister is a sister, and sisterhood is powerful wherever you're lucky enough to find it.

Queen of the Road

"Do I have to go?" I whine to Flash in a voice not unlike a three-year-old's.

"Yes, you have to go," my beloved replies.

We are sitting side by side in the Lesbianville International Airport, waiting for my flight to be called. I am off on a two-week coast-to-coast all-expenses-paid book tour, complete with an at-your-service escort in every city. "All you have to do," my publisher told me, "is wake up and put on your make-up. We'll take care of the rest." At last I have a chance to become accustomed to the life I've become accustomed to not becoming accustomed to!

So why am I so glum? Because A) there are no conjugal visits on my tour, and B) I have to put 30,000 feet between my purple platform pumps and the ground thirteen times in the next fourteen days. And I'm one of those people who think flying is for the birds.

To calm my gay nerves, I hum "Leaving on a Jet Plane" over and over until my beloved pokes me in the ribs. Then I switch to "Wind Beneath My Wings." Finally, much to Flash's relief, my flight starts to board. We walk to the gate and kiss good-bye for the eighty-seventh time.

"Don't forget to write," Flash calls, waving.

"I won't." I wave back. "I've got a book review to edit, a poem to finish…"

"To me," Flash yells over the engines. "Don't forget to write *to me.*"

"I won't," I shout, but as I am already on board, I doubt my darling can hear me.

I hurry down the aisle, glancing at my ticket. My seat number is 36B, which also happens to be my bra size, a sure sign from the Goddess that both my Maidenform and I will survive this trip intact.

I sit down, buckle up, and pray that soon I'll be safely above the clouds with no one sitting near me. They may call them the Friendly Skies, but I, for one, detest rubbing auras with people I've never met before. Men like to make passes. Women like to make conversation. I like to pretend I don't speak English, but I usually blow my own cover by pointing to the roll on my neighbor's lunch tray and asking, "Excuse me, are you going to eat that?"

Unfortunately, today's flight is filling up and spilling over, and sure enough, here comes a burly man in a business suit who clearly has dibs on 36A, the window seat. I stand to let him by and watch as he sinks down, buckles up, and spreads his legs as far as they will go, like a perfect Pap smear patient.

Before I can take my seat again, someone taps me on the shoulder. "Is this 36C?" I turn to see a nun who barely comes up to my armpits studying her ticket. Now our little row is complete, with yours truly squashed between the Sister and the Suit.

"Are you traveling for business or pleasure?" asks the Suit.

"Business," I answer. "I'm on a book tour."

"Isn't that nice," says the Sister, patting my knee. "What's the name of your book, dear?"

"*My Lover Is a Woman*," I brag as the businessman snaps his legs shut.

"You don't say." The nun leans forward. "You know, my ex-lover is a woman."

"Really?" I lean forward too. "My lover is an ex-nun."

"Small world," says the nun as we both lean back for takeoff. Everything goes smoothly, and soon the two fags in front of us aren't the only ones cruising at 15,000 feet.

A short time later our Domestic Flight Goddess appears with her cart. "Something to drink?" she asks the businessman. He takes tomato juice. "Something to drink?" she asks the nun. She orders bourbon. "It's a nasty habit," the nun explains, downing the shot in one gulp. The Domestic Flight Goddess hands her another and turns to me. "How would you like to visit the Great Mall in the Sky?"

"Excuse me?"

"You go, girl," says the flying nun, tossing back her booze. Then she points out the window. "Hey, is that Cloud Nine?"

"The Great Mall in the Sky," I repeat. That can mean only one thing, but before I can protest that I'm not yet ready to meet my maker, the Domestic Flight Goddess hands me a shopping catalog thicker than all sixty-nine volumes of the *Encyclopedia Lesbiannica* put together. Talk about heaven!

"Use the phone in your armrest to place your order," the DFG says. "Calls are only a dollar a minute." Just like therapy! Another happy coincidence. I proceed to shop 'til we drop down in San Francisco, five hours and hundreds of dollars later.

"Hi, I'm Java." A butch in leather pants greets me at the gate. "Do you have luggage?"

Do *I* have luggage? Does Heather have two mommies? We head for Baggage Claim, where suitcases are already circling. "That's mine," I say, pointing to the carousel. "And that one. And that one. And those two. And that one. And that one."

"You have seven bags for a fourteen-day trip?" Java is amazed.

"I know. Flash couldn't believe it either," I tell her. "She thought I'd need at least sixteen."

Java swallows her butch pride and goes in search of a luggage cart. We load up and head for her car.

"So what's the plan?" I ask as we pull onto the highway. "Any time for sight-seeing?"

"Sight-seeing?" Java gives me a look. "You have interviews at one, two, three, four, five, and six o'clock, not to mention a reading at seven-thirty."

"Oh, my God." I give Java a look. "When do I eat?"

"Whenever you can."

"Do we have time to stop at the hotel?" I ask. "I was hoping for a nap."

"Do you have jet lag?" Java asks. "I have just the thing."

Thank God for California girls! Of course she has some natural, herbal, vegetarian, chem-free, wheat-free, dairy-free, sugar-free, yeast-free, taste-free poultice/tincture/tablet/sprout that will give me an energy boost. Java reaches under her seat, pulls out a coffeepot, and plugs it in to the socket where her cigarette lighter should be. "Caffeine," she says. "It's the only way to go." I down a cup while Java makes a sharp U-turn and pulls into a parking place.

We whip from interview to interview, and I tell where, when, why, how, and for whom the book was written over and over, trying to dazzle each reporter with my spontaneous wit, never letting on that I've been asked the exact same questions and given the exact same answers a hundred times before. As the day goes by, I actually grow sick of the sound of my own voice, a phenomenon I'm sure Flash would be pleased to hear about, except, of course, I'll never tell her.

Finally Java takes me to my hotel, where I have a full fifteen minutes to wash, dry, brush, fluff, powder, puff, and pour myself into a red-and-black minidress Fran Drescher would die for. Then I rush downstairs, get back into Java's car, and off we go to the reading.

"Hi, I'm Page, the bookstore owner. Welcome to Clit Lit." Page has green hair, a vulva tattooed on her left cheek, and earlobes that look like Swiss cheese. She takes me to the back of the store where an eager audience is assembled, including the nun from seat 36C, who's wearing a motorcycle jacket, freedom rings, and a dog collar over her habit. She waves, and I wave back. Then Page introduces me, and I take my place behind the podium. But wait. Something's wrong.

"Psst, Java," I whisper.

"What's the matter?" she whispers back.

"Give me a leg up."

"Why?"

"Because," I say, placing my five-inch heel in her hand, "butches have been putting me up on pedestals for years. And besides," I add, hopping into the air, "I spent half my advance on this outfit, and no one can see it." I pirouette on the lectern, and the girls go wild. Then I clear my throat, shield my eyes from the glare of the lights reflected in all those earrings, chin rings, cheek rings, lip rings, lid rings, brow rings, and tongue rings, and begin to read. I finish with a flourish, but before I can even cop a curtsy, Java whisks me away.

"What's the hurry?" I ask.

"More interviews," she says, hustling me to the car. "You've got one at eight, nine, ten, and eleven o'clock, not to mention a talk show at midnight."

"But I'm so tired." I can't help but whine.

"Here, have some candy." Java hands me a bag.

"Thanks." I pour some into my mouth. "What are these, Milk Duds?"

"No. They're chocolate-covered espresso beans."

Zing! I whip through the rest of the interviews in no time at all and then bid Java good night in front of my hotel.

Upstairs, inside my room, I bypass the bed and head straight for the matching fainting couch beside it. Once deposited, I pick up the phone and call Flash.

"Hi–how–are–you–I–love–you–I–miss–you–I–want–you–I–need–you–did–I–get–any–voice–mail–snail–mail–E–mail–fax–mail–how's–the–weather–can–I–talk–to–the–cat?"

"Do you know what time it is?" My beloved speaks slowly, as if she's zonked out on quaaludes.

"Yeah, it's one o'clock. So it's ten o'clock your time, right?"

"Wrong," Flash groans. "It's three o'clock in the morning."

"Oh, my God, did I wake you?"

"No, the phone did. So how's the Brunette Ambition Tour going?"

"Oh, Flash, it's fabulous. San Francisco is fabulous, the girls are fabulous, the hotel is fabulous, my hair is fabulous…"

"Whoa." Flash pauses to catch her breath from listening so fast. "How many cups of coffee did you drink today?"

My beloved knows me so well. "I don't know — I lost count after twenty-three. Why?"

"Because you sound like Mariah Carey on helium."

I take that as a compliment and continue babbling away. After an hour we hang up, and I sink into the sheets of my king-size bed. Just as my head hits the pillow, the phone rings. "Who died?" I yell into the receiver.

"This is your wake-up call," says an automated voice that sounds just like *Star Trek: Voyager*'s Captain Janeway. I leap out of bed, fabulize myself, and race downstairs where Java is waiting to take me to the airport. I hop onto the plane and hop off several hours later.

"Hi, I'm Mocha," says my new escort, and we're off and running.

Thirteen days, twelve cities, and 200 interviews later, I arrive back in Lesbianville so tired, I stagger right past my beloved, who is waiting with flowers at the gate.

"Yoo-hoo," calls a voice that sounds vaguely familiar. "Aren't you the author of *My Lover Is a Woman*?"

"My lover is a woman," I tell my handsome butch, "but your lover is chopped liver."

"Just what I'm in the mood for," Flash says, nibbling my left ear and taking me home to devour.

Silence = Sleep

"**R**oll over, Flash," I command, giving my beloved a gentle yet firm push.

Now don't be shocked, dear reader. I am not about to describe, in vivid detail or otherwise, the lurid sex acts that Flash and I indulge in (and whether she's a rollover butch or not is a secret that will follow me to the grave). No, in fact at this very moment Flash is sound asleep. So why am I insisting that she dream on her left side instead of her right? Am I that much of a control queen? Of course I am, but that's beside the point.

The point is, Flash is snoring. She has just awakened me from my favorite Martina dream: I am on the tennis court in a beaded sleeveless white minidress, with sequined sneakers on my feet. Martina comes up behind me, circling my waist with her left hand. With her right hand she holds my wrist and shows me how to swing. My racket clatters to the ground as she turns me toward her, holds me close, and whispers in that to-die-for accent, "Lesléa..."

All of a sudden my dream changes. I am in a truck, driving over a bridge, the kind that makes your wheels vibrate really loudly. I drive over the bridge again. And again. And again. The noise is unbearable. My eyes snap open, but the noise is still there. It's coming from my beloved.

"Flash." No response. "Flash!" How can she sleep through this commotion? It sounds like a dozen dykes are in the room with us trying out their chain saws. "*Flash!*" I scream, but of course she can't hear me. Who could with all this noise?

Desperate times call for desperate action. Thank God, I have a secret weapon: my feet. I'm the type of gal whose feet instantly become thirty degrees colder than the rest of my body the second I hit the bed. I whip off my wool socks and plant my ice-cold tootsies on the warm, unsuspecting back of my sleeping beloved.

"Mgwfth!" Flash scoots away from me, makes a weird chewing noise, and, thank the Goddess, turns over. The sounds of silence fill our bedroom. I put my socks back on and shut my eyes. Soon I am deep in another recurring dream: k.d. lang is onstage singing "Constant Craving." She looks out into the audience. Our eyes meet. She beckons with her finger, and I float over the rest of her shrieking fans until I am onstage beside her. k.d. stands behind me and puts her arms around my waist. She croons into my ear and then turns me toward her, holding me close. " Lesléa," she whispers in time to the music. "Lesléa…"

All of a sudden my dream changes. I am pushing a lawn mower, its engine louder than a Boeing 747. I mow the same strip of grass again. And again. And again. "Flash!" I keep my eyes shut just in case k.d. decides to come back, but she is gone, as are any hopes of getting a good night's sleep.

Morning finds Flash singing in the shower and me barely able to crawl out of bed. My beloved leaves for work, and after eight cups of coffee I manage to drag myself to my desk, where I immediately fall asleep.

Flash finds me with my head pillowed on my computer when she comes home for lunch. She shakes my shoulder. "Are you okay?" she asks. "Why are you so tired?"

"Take three guesses, and the first two don't count," I say.

Flash looks at me, puzzled. Sarcasm is not my usual style (it's so unladylike). But sleep deprivation does strange things to a girl. I decide to level with her. "Flash, you snored all night."

"I *snored*?" She is shocked and insulted, as if I have just accused her of doing something utterly preposterous, like leaving the house without her daily dab of Brylcreem. She shakes her head and gives a little laugh. "I don't snore."

I am too tired to argue with her, so the matter is dropped — until midnight, when her snores interrupt my favorite Madonna dream, the one in which the Material Girl and I justify our love. This is really the last straw. I storm out of bed and return with a tape recorder, which I place on the headboard.

The next morning I present Flash with exhibit A: a tape of her nightly serenade.

"That's me?" Flash listens intently. "That can't be me."

"Well, it certainly isn't my mother." Another sleepless night has not improved my mood.

"It's not like I snore on purpose," Flash says. "And besides, you can sleep through a thunderstorm, two cats purring in stereo on either side of your head, and the smoke alarm going off all at the same time. Why can't you sleep through my snoring?"

"It's not like I wake up on purpose," I snap back. "Just leave me alone." Flash goes to take her shower, and I hang a DO NOT DISTURB sign on my big toe and try to get some shut-eye. But it's no use. I'm too much of a workaholic to sleep away the day. But I'm also too tired to get any work done. So what's a girl to do? Why, go shopping, of course.

First I buy a pair of black shoes to match the bags under my eyes. Then I go to the drugstore to pick up a few items.

Back home Flash wants to know what's in the packages. "Oh, just some things for bedtime," I say nonchalantly.

Flash lets out a tremendous yawn. "I'm *really* tired. Can we go to bed now?" she asks, her voice full of hope and excitement. This is because the last time I brought home some bags for bedtime they contained ben-wa balls, edible underwear, and a naughty nightie. Tonight I am also full of surprises.

"Lie down," I croon to Flash. "Shut your eyes." My darling does as she's told, licking her lips in anticipation. I rip open several packages, and before Flash can protest I pop a Snore No More pillow under her head, prop open her nostrils with nasal tape, slip an anti-snoring ring up her nose, and attach a Snore Busters devise onto her arm that emits a small electroshock every time she makes a sound.

"What the hell?" Flash opens her frightened eyes. "Are we into S/M now? Ouch!" Flash's questions have elicited several shocks to her arm. "I can't sleep like this," she says, removing all her hardware. "Look, I brought you something too." Flash hands me a little box.

"What's this?" I ask coyly. Flash and I fight so rarely, she can usually afford to make up with me rather extravagantly.

"Just a little something for your ears," Flash says, nibbling on my left lobe.

"Oh, Flash." I melt, instantly ready to forgive her. Flash knows the way to this femme's heart is jewelry. I envision diamond studs, dangling rubies, pearl posts perhaps. But what I see when I open the box really takes my breath away. "Earplugs?" I shriek. "You think I'm going to sleep with earplugs?"

"Why not?" Clearly Flash thinks she has come up with the perfect solution.

"Because," I sputter, "my mother told me never to put anything except my elbows into my ears."

"And since when do you listen to your mother?" Flash asks.

"That's beside the point." I fling the earplugs onto the bed. "There's only one thing left to do, Flash. We're going to pay a little visit to Sapphrodite."

"Who's Sapphrodite?"

I look at my beloved as if she's just said, *Who's Cher?* "Sapphrodite is the goddess of couples counseling." I lower my voice in reverence. "Don't you remember the article she wrote about that couple — one woman was such a separatist, she wouldn't even have a Mr. Coffee in the house, and the other woman had three teenage sons — and after only a few sessions they worked everything out and lived happily ever after?"

Flash is not impressed. "How much does this goddess charge?"

"Oh, she's very reasonable," I say, keeping my voice light. "Only $150 an hour."

"What!"

"Flash!" I glare at her. "Look me right in the eye and tell me you wouldn't spend seventy-five bucks to save our marriage."

Flash looks me right in the eye — and admits defeat.

Our appointment with Sapphrodite is the following Saturday. Flash and I have taken turns sleeping on the couch all week, and neither one of us is in a very good mood. We drive to Sapphrodite's office in silence, enter her waiting room, and sit as far from each other as we possibly can. Flash reads a magazine, and I look out the window. It is an exceptionally gorgeous day, and I can think of about 8,000 things I'd rather be doing. I sigh and shut my eyes. All of a sudden my ears fill with the sound of a steady rainfall, lulling me into a light sleep. Then my eyes snap open. How can it be raining when the sky is as blue as my eye shadow? Am I losing my mind?

"Flash," I say, turning to my beloved. "Do you see any rain out there?"

Flash looks up from the September issue of *Popular Dyke Mechanics*. "No."

"Then why does it sound like rain?"

Flash listens. "That's strange," she says. She looks around the waiting room and points to a small round alien-looking object right out of *Star Trek: Deep Space Nine*. "It's coming from that," she says, going over to investigate.

Flash pushes a button, and the sound of rain is replaced by a thumping heartbeat. She pushes another button, and we hear wind rustling through leaves. She pushes another button, and we hear a distraught female voice shrieking, "You slept with her in *our* bed? With Fluffy watching?"

"Whoops, must have hit the OFF switch," Flash says, hitting another button, which fills the room with whale noises.

"That's it! Flash, don't you see?" I am beside myself with excitement. "It's a noise-drowner-outer. We'll just get one of these to drown out your snoring."

But Flash is two steps ahead of me. She's already unplugged the thing and stuffed it into my pocketbook.

"But, Flash," I whisper, "that's stealing."

"Not if you leave 150 bucks. I'm sure these don't cost a penny over $99.99."

I hastily write out the check, and then we make a break for it. In no time at all we are fleeing down the highway in Flash's car.

When we get home my darling plugs in our new toy. We lie in bed listening to the soothing sounds of ocean waves crashing to shore. "Roll over, Flash," I murmur.

"I'm not snoring," she says defensively.

"Who said anything about snoring?" I ask, giving my beloved a gentle yet firm push. She takes the hint, and we spend the next several hours blissfully celebrating the salvation of our marriage. Then, arms and legs entwined, we both fall into a much-needed and well-deserved sleep.

The Way We Purr

"We are gathered here this afternoon to mourn and to celebrate the nine lives of Couscous Kerouac..."

"Come back, little Cousy, come back," I shriek, throwing myself on top of her size-10 triple-E shoe box of a coffin.

"There, there." Flash gathers me up in her arms and strokes my back, but I am beyond comfort. Now that Cousy has joined PC in the Great Litter Box in the Sky, Flash and I are a feline-free family. Which is a sorry state of affairs, because, let's face it, a lesbian without a pussy is like, well, a lesbian without a pussy.

What to do? I schedule an emergency session with my therapist and spend the entire fifty-minute hour crying (luckily, a dollar a minute includes a tissue a minute).

Raven drops by and tries to put me in a good mood with compliments: "That's a fabulous sweater. Did you just get it?"

"Raven, this sweater is older than you are."

"Really? It looks new. Oh, I know what it is. It has no cat hair on it."

"It doesn't?" I wail. So much for cheering me up.

Weeks pass, but my grief does not. I cry not only for Cousy but also for all the pets I have loved and lost: Chirpy the parakeet, who flew the coop one afternoon as I watched *Bye Bye Birdie;* Mr. and Mrs. Moishe Goldfish, whom I carried home in a Ziploc bag belly-up; and Agnes of Dog, my one and only puppy love. *If I learned to live without them,* I tell myself, *I can learn to live without Cousy.*

But I don't believe me, for months later I still find myself sobbing in the supermarket in front of the Friskies Chicken and Tuna Delight display. I still play the original cast album of *Cats* every night after supper, much to Flash's dismay. "Do we have to hear that now?"

"And forever," I say, turning up the volume. Then I take out Cousy's photo album and make Flash stroll down memory lane with me. There's Baby Cousy chasing her tail and Crone Cousy asleep in the sun. There's Femme-Top Cousy with a rhinestone-studded black velvet collar and Jock Cousy scaling the heights of the furniture. There's Cousy getting in touch with her inner kitty, nursing on my cashmere sweater, and Cousy getting in touch with her inner bitch, biting the hand that feeds her (I still have the scar).

We look at photos of Country Cousy chasing a field mouse and City Cousy chasing a rat. There's Hippie Cousy growing her own catnip and Punk Cousy, her fur sticking up straight in a Mohawk. There's Separatist Cousy hissing at Raven and Activist Cousy, a red ribbon pinned to her collar. There's even a picture of Couscous the Bulimic Wonder, barfing her dinner back into her bowl.

Looking at all these pictures of Cousy exhausts me, so I lie down for a little catnap. As soon as I shut my eyes, I feel something sharp, like a claw, digging into my ankle. I turn around just in time to see a run traveling up my stocking faster than the speed of light — and I see Couscous, looking quite proud, with something small and furry in her mouth. I shriek and jump onto a chair. What is it this time: a mole, a bat, a squirrel? I place my hand over my eyes and peer down through my fingers. "Oh, my God," I gasp, "a kitten." I hop down and pick up the little ball of fur. It immediately nestles into my neck and begins to purr. "Cousy, where did you get her?" I ask, but Couscous is gone, and I am awake, telling Flash the dream.

The very next day I call our vet, Dr. Dykelittle, and ask her if she has any kittens to adopt. "Someone brought in a stray this morning," she says. "Would you like to come see her?"

"We'll be right there." I call Flash at work and tell her to fake a migraine. She's home in a minute, and we get to the vet in two seconds flat.

"Here she is," Dr. Dykelittle says, depositing a small ball of long white fur in my arms. The kitten immediately nestles into my neck and with one swipe of her claw not only draws blood but also destroys the diamond necklace Flash bought me for my fortieth birthday.

"What a sweet cat," I croon, scratching her under the chin.

"We've been calling her Princess," Dr. Dykelittle says, wiping my wound with an alcohol pad.

"We've got to change her name," I tell Flash when we're back in the car. "There's only room for one Princess in this family."

The Cat Formerly Known as Princess agrees, for she takes on the role of *queen* the minute she sets paw in the house. When she decides the only place suitable for a catnap is my pink angora sweater, I don't argue with her. When she discovers the best scratching post in the house is the leg of Flash's antique oak table, I sprinkle catnip on it to make it more enticing. When she makes it clear that the only bowl she will lower herself to eat from is my grandmother's cut-glass crystal, I apologize for not offering the family heirloom sooner.

Flash and I are crazy about this kitten. In two days we take 200 pictures of her. We spend most of the time rolling around the kitchen floor, not with each other but with our beloved baby. We wake up joyfully for the 2:00 A.M. feeding, the 4:00 A.M. feeding, the 6:00 A.M. feeding. Dykes stop me on the street and comment on my sleepless but satisfied look. "Are you in love?" they ask.

"Yes," I happily answer.

But while I am ecstatic, Flash isn't quite sure that the Cat Formerly Known as Princess is content. I think she seems happy enough, chewing on the sleeves of my suede jacket and shredding the shower curtain, but my beloved remains doubtful. "I don't know," Flash says one night as I polish my nails and the Cat Formerly Known as Princess's claws Pussy Pink. "Maybe she needs a playmate."

"She has two playmates," I say, pointing at myself and Flash with the tiny nail-polish brush.

"No, I mean a brother or a sister." Flash folds her arms. "I was an only child," she reminds me, "and I always wanted a sibling."

"I had a sibling," I remind Flash, "and I always wanted to be an only child."

Flash shrugs her shoulders and retires to the living room to watch *Lifestyles of the Butch and Famous* while I put a topcoat on the Cat Formerly Known as Princess's toes. Then in a flash I see what the problem is: Our new kitty isn't lonely — *Flash* is lonely. Two femme tops and one bashful butch equals an unbalanced household. Flash couldn't agree more.

The next day the Great Cat Hunt begins. I call everyone I know and finally find a lead: Mitzi's roommate's therapist's therapist's roommate knows a dyke named Kitty whose cat has kittens every six months or so. I call her immediately. "Do you have any kittens to spare?" I ask.

"Just one," she says.

"We'll be right there."

I call Flash at work and tell her to tell her boss she has cramps. "But she knows I'm going through menopause," Flash says, always paying too much attention to details. Luckily, Flash's boss is also going through menopause, and her memory isn't what it used to be. Flash makes the great escape, picks me up, and off we go.

"C'mon in," Kitty says. "The kitten's in there." She leads us into the living room, where a little Morris-like redhead is tearing some lace curtains to bits.

"Oh, what a pretty, witty, itty-bitty kitty," my boot-stomping butch squeals through clenched teeth, her voice suddenly high enough to make my contact lenses crack. The kitten chirps something equally incoherent in reply.

"He just discovered his meow yesterday," Kitty tells us. "He's been singing all day."

Flash promptly names her pal New Cat on the Block and proves her undying love for him by putting all our lives in danger and letting me drive home so she can cuddle her kitten in her lap. I pull into the driveway, and Flash carries New Cat on the Block into the house and presents him to his sister. I'm afraid the Cat Formerly Known as Princess will hiss, scratch, or bite, but instead she goes wild with excitement. She leaps into the air with glee, runs toward her new little brother, and then dashes away to the bedroom. He gallops after her, and a minute later both kittens run past me and Flash into the kitchen, this time New Cat on the Block in the lead. They thunder through the apartment like little horses for hours, running, leaping, prancing, dancing, and doing triple toe loops in the air that would make Tonya Harding proud.

Flash and I are so in love with these kittens, our friends are a little worried about us. Flash cuts her hours at work to half-time so she can be home with our babies more. I cancel a fifteen-city book tour because I can't bear the thought of being away from our little darlings that long. But our friends don't even know the half of it. We haven't had sex in weeks because Flash is afraid it will upset the children.

"Maybe they could sleep in the living room tonight," I dare to suggest.

"Have you lost your mind?" Flash says, glaring at me.

"Well, then shut the light."

"I can't," Flash says. "New Cat on the Block is sleeping on my arm. You shut the light."

"I can't get up. The Cat Formerly Known as Princess is asleep on my chest." I lift the covers to show Flash.

"Oh, look at the burly, curly, twirly, pearly, surly girly," Flash squeaks in a falsetto that sounds like a cross between Minnie Mouse and Melanie Griffith.

Suddenly a lightbulb goes on over my head. "Flash," I say with a kittenish peep, "wouldn't you like some pretty titty and itty-bitty clitty?"

"There's too many pussies in this bed," Flash growls in a low Tina Turner "Private Dancer" kind of voice. We remedy the situation, and soon all the pussies in the house are satisfied and sound asleep.

The Taming of the Screw

All's quiet on the writing front. I've given Flash a kiss she'll taste all day and shooed her off to work. The Cat Formerly Known as Princess and New Cat on the Block have finished destroying my pink feather boa and matching mules and have fallen asleep in the sun. Nothing can stop me from writing the Great American Lesbian Novel now. I pick up my Bic and…the phone rings.

"Who can that be?" I ask, annoyed. It's only 9:37. I've told everyone I know not to call me before noon. This is my writing time, for God's sake. What inconsiderate oaf has the nerve to call me during the peak hours of my creativity? Why, my mother, of course.

"So how are you?" she asks.

"Ma, I can't talk now. I'm working."

"You got a job?" Her voice rises with delight.

"No, Ma. I'm writing."

"Oh, you're writing." Her voice plummets. "I thought you said you were working."

"I am working."

"Oh, you're working? I thought you were writing."

"I am writing."

"You're writing? I thought you were working."

"I am work — " I interrupt our little Abbott and Costello routine and ask her in a brusque can't-you-see-I'm-busy tone of voice, "Ma, what's up?"

"I'm calling to ask you what I should get Flash for Chanukah."

"Ma, I don't know how to break it to you," I say, choosing my words carefully, "but Flash isn't Jewish."

"I know Flash isn't Jewish," my mother says in an as-if-I-could-ever-forget-why-don't-you-stick-the-knife-into-my-heart-farther-and-twist-it tone of voice. "I can still buy her a Chanukah present. She won't care — a present is a present." For someone who has talked to Flash only half a dozen times in her entire life, my mother knows my girlfriend awfully well.

"Ma, we don't really celebrate the holidays." Well, that's not exactly true. On Chanukah we light the menorah and play strip dreidel, and on Christmas we put the Party Dykes CD *O Little Town of Lesbianville* on the stereo and spend a few hours under the mistletoe. But I don't think I'll tell my mother that.

"So," she continues, "I was thinking of getting her a nice blouse."

"Ma, Flash doesn't wear blouses. She wears shirts."

"Skirts? Oh, that's a good idea. A nice skirt. They're wearing them just below the knee this year."

"Ma, I don't think clothes are a good idea."

"How about jewelry then? What about a nice necklace?"

What's with the "nice"? Flash doesn't even have a nice girl-friend. I'm sure she will be less than interested in a nice neck-lace, especially as it would clash with the nasty necklace she's worn around her neck for the past twenty-five years: a three-inch labrys she never removes except to sharpen its blades when the moon is full. "Um, I don't think so."

"Well, what does she need?"

Impatience makes me blurt out the truth: "Money."

"Money?" My mother sounds puzzled, as if she's never heard of it.

"Yeah, money. You know: dough, bread, bills, loot, cash, greenbacks, gelt..."

"I can't send Flash money." My mother is shocked at the very idea. "That's so *impersonal*."

"Ma, you send me money every year."

"You? That's different." My mother thinks for a minute. "I know. I'll send you a check, and you buy her something from me. You know what she likes."

That's personal? "I don't have time to do your holiday shopping, Ma. I have to get back to work."

"You got a job?"

"Ma!"

"All right, all right. Listen, think about it and call me back. And don't tell Flash. I want it to be a surprise."

I hang up the phone and immediately call Flash. "Listen, my mother wants to get you a Chanukah present."

Flash is stunned. "You still haven't told her I'm not Jewish?"

"Of course I told her. She wants to get you a Chanukah present anyway."

"Well, I guess that's okay. I mean, I don't care. A present is a present."

"So what do you want?"

"Money."

"I tried that already. She doesn't want to send you money."

"But she always sends *you* money," Flash whines like one of the Smothers Brothers. "Mom always liked you better."

"Just think about it and let me know so I can call her back."

I hang up the phone and pick up my Bic. But instead of going back to Chapter 12 of *My Daughter the Dyke,* my mind is now focused on the holidays. I don't know what to tell my mother to buy for Flash. Flash is very hard to buy for. Now, if my mother had asked what *I* wanted for Chanukah, I could have given her a list longer than RuPaul's arm: anything with rhinestones, rubies, diamonds, emeralds, amethysts, opals, or pearls. Anything made of silk, satin, cashmere, mohair, taffeta, tulle, or lace. Flash, on the other hand, would be satisfied with anything held together with nails, screws, nuts, bolts, batteries, glue, or duct tape. Anything made of wood, metal, plastic, fiberglass, sawdust, Sheetrock, or vinyl.

How can I ever explain to my mother that the way to a butch's heart is through her tool belt? Actually, believe it or not, this *is* something my mother would understand. They say necessity is the mother of invention, but my mother found it necessary to invent ways to keep the house from falling apart because she married a man who spent day after day playing with his one and only six-inch tool: a butter knife.

My mother, on the other hand, believes there's no tool like an old tool and has spent decades filling the kitchen drawers with hammers, screwdrivers, wrenches, pliers, paintbrushes, sandpaper, and T squares. My mother is known around the neighborhood as Mrs. Fix Up or Shut Up. I remember one summer afternoon long ago when little Binky Shmendrick got his foot caught in his bicycle between the pedal and the frame. Mrs. Shmendrick called the fire department, but before the truck even left the station, my mother had taken apart Binky's bicycle, put it back together, and raised the seat two inches like Binky had been asking his father to do for years.

Now that I think about it, the last time Flash and I visited my parents, my mother dazzled my darling with her cordless screwdriver. While my father and I defied gender roles by donning matching aprons and whipping up a soufflé, Flash helped my mother take apart and reassemble an entire bookcase that needed its shelves readjusted. "Your wife is a whiz at screwing," Flash had said with great admiration to my father, who, fortunately, had his hearing aid turned down at the time.

I pick up the phone and call my mother back. "Listen, I know the perfect present for you to buy Flash. A cordless screwdriver."

"A cordless screwdriver?"

"Yeah, you know, like yours."

"What kind of present is a cordless screwdriver?" my mother asks. "I wanted to get her something nice, you know, like a sweater set."

A sweater set? Even *I* don't wear sweater sets. Suddenly I see what my mother is doing. Since I didn't turn out to be the daughter she's always wanted, she thinks she has a second chance with Flash. "Ma," I say, my tone serious, "do you want to buy Flash a present that will make you happy or a present that will make Flash happy?" I hold my breath as the question floats in the air and my entire childhood flashes before my eyes.

"A cordless screwdriver?" my mother muses out loud.

"She'll love it. Trust me." Uh-oh. Wrong thing to say. I haven't said those two little words since I was fifteen and wanted to convince my mother to leave me alone for the weekend. She and my father came home earlier than expected only to find me and Binky Shmendrick dressed in two of my mother's evening gowns, smoking pot out of my father's pipe and eating sandwiches filled with Bosco and Fluffernutter.

I don't think about our conversation again until a week later when a package arrives for Flash. "It's from your mother," Flash says, ripping open the carton. My beloved gasps in ecstasy at what she finds inside. "Quick," she yells, "get me something to screw."

"At your service," I say, unbuttoning my blouse.

Flash ignores me and attacks the telephone table with passion. Then she goes through the entire house tightening bookcases, doorknobs, table legs, bureau drawers, chair backs, cabinets, and shelves.

Hours later, when everything in the house has been screwed except *moi,* I hand an exhausted Flash the cordless phone. "Don't you think you should call my mother?" I ask my beloved.

She dials and barely waits for someone to answer. "I've screwed everything in sight today," she shouts, "including your daughter!"

"Flash!" I lunge for the phone.

"Relax, I got a busy signal." My darling hangs up and takes me in her arms. "This was your doing, wasn't it?" she asks, giving me a grateful kiss. Just as I slip my hands under her tool belt, the phone rings.

"Cordless interruptus," I murmur, reaching for the receiver. It's my mother, wanting to know how Flash likes her present.

"She's screwing?" my mother asks.

"She's screwing," I pant.

"Happy Chanukah," my mother says. "May you both screw in good health for many years to come."

Amen.

First Family Values

Flash and I are browsing in Queer Shlock, our favorite tchotchke shop, when my beloved looks up from the labia-shaped lampshade she's admiring and asks, "Hey, isn't that Eleanor Roosevelt?"

I glance up from the book I'm reading and follow Flash's finger out the window. The woman she's pointing to does look like Eleanor, but how can that be? Maybe I'm having a flashback? (I dropped acid in the sixties, but I never swallowed.) Or perhaps my middle-aged eyes are playing tricks on me. I squint into the distance, and suddenly I see the light.

"That's not Eleanor Roosevelt," I tell Flash. "That's Chelsea Clinton."

"Chelsea Clinton!"

We race out of the shlock shop and into the street, where a small crowd has gathered. "Is it really Hillary and the Chels?" I ask Snoop, our local Brenda Starr.

"It's them all right." Snoop is frantically scribbling in her notebook. "They're checking out the local college scene. Rumor has it Chelsea has applied to Dyke U."

Dyke University, my old alma mater? Oh, this is too good to be true.

"Hey, what's that you're reading?" Snoop, ever the snoop, asks.

"You forgot to pay for it," Flash, ever the Girl Scout, reminds me.

"Whoops."

I hold up the book for Snoop to inspect. "*How Would You Feel If Your Dad Was Gay?*" she reads from the cover.

"Hey, speaking of dads," I say, "how do you think Billy Boy would feel if the First Daughter was gay?"

"Why don't you ask him?" Flash asks.

"Good idea," I say, and that night I compose a letter.

Dear Mr. President:

Well, I was simply delighted to catch a glimpse of the First Lady and the First Offspring right here in our little town of Lesbianville! How exciting to see the First Family, sans Papa, strolling down the streets of our fair city! Tell me, is it true, Mr. Prez, that you may be sending the First Teenager to the Land of Lesbos to receive an education? I am just dripping at the thought. Now, now, Billy Boy, don't have a cow. It's not your darling daughter I'm all shook up about. Unlike the Lesbian Avengers, I do not recruit. No, what floats my boat is the thought of all those Secret Service dykes protecting the Wee One. Oh, how I do love a lady in uniform!

As I stood in the crowd all a-tremble, Bill, I realized, in my haste to see the chief executrix, I had forgotten to pay for the book I still clutched in my hand, a children's book called *How Would You Feel If Your Dad Was Gay?*

Which is what prompted this letter, oh Fearful Leader. What I want to know is this: How would you feel if your daughter was gay?

Now, before I am hung up by my bra straps for outing the First Teenager, let me assure you, Mr. Clinton (any relation to Kate?), that I know nothing about Chelsea's sexual proclivities. She was here for such a short period of time, I didn't ask, and she didn't tell. But let's just give her the benefit of the doubt. Let's just say Chelsea is lucky enough to grow up to be a happy homo like *moi*. What will her life be like?

The first thing Chelsea does, to the cheers of every gay boy in the nation, is cut her hair. She looks so adorable in her new do that she instantly meets the grrrl of her dreams. The grrrl is kind, gentle, sexy, sweet, and strong enough to stomach the fact that her girlfriend's very own father signed a bill into law that prevented his own daughter from being legally wed.

Let's say Chelsea and her Amazon (whom we'll call Babe) settle down and decide to raise a family. (It takes a village to find a sperm donor.) Little Tyke is born, and everyone is happy. For a while. Then Chelsea loses her job because she's a lesbian (as I'm sure you know, Mr. Prez, the antidiscrimination bill did not pass). Chelsea is all stressed out, tensions mount in the marital bed, and Babe decides to take little Tyke home to mother. Babe also decides that Chelsea is not really Tyke's parent, and Chelsea goes to court.

Unfortunately the judge deems Chelsea a "biological stranger" to the child, and grants her no custodial or visitation rights. But don't despair, Willie. Our heartbroken heroine is young, she's resilient, she falls in love again. This time she makes sure no babies are in the picture. Doll is just not the maternal type.

Chelsea is in seventh heaven until Doll falls ill with a mysterious disease. Her parents whisk her off to a treatment center and don't allow Chelsea near their darling daughter. Again

Chelsea takes to the courts, and again a judge decides she is not immediate family. Chelsea is devastated. In despair she decides to join the military, but since all her trials and tribulations have been in the tabloids, she's as good as told. So, what's a girl to do?

Well, you know what I always say: When in doubt, hire an agent. Chelsea writes her memoirs, a book called *First Dyke,* which sells over a million copies. The book is translated into forty-seven languages. It becomes a movie, a play, a musical, a sitcom. Chelsea becomes rich and famous and a regular on *The Rosie O'Donnell Show.* Oh, wait, that's not Chelsea's life. That's my life. In my dreams.

Anyway, Mr. Bill, the point is, November 5th has come and gone. And on the same day my fellow Americans decided you were going to rule the roost for the next four years, I turned forty-one. So even though you didn't ask, I'm going to tell you what I'd like for my birthday (there's always next year): I wouldn't mind some cash, which is something a lesbian writer can always use. Short of that, my birthday wishes are these: I want to be able to walk down the street holding Flash's hand without being afraid that such a simple show of affection will result in a broken jaw. I want my marriage to be legally recognized. I want health insurance. I want hospital visitation rights. I want my friends to stop worrying about losing their kids and their jobs. I want my friends who want to join the military to be able to do so. In short, I want my civil rights. And I want them now. Lest you forget, First Father, I am somebody's daughter too.

Yours for four more,
Lesléa

"So what do you think, Flash?" I ask my beloved after reading her my letter.

"Another document for your FBI file," she says, shaking her head.

"Think he'll answer me?" I ask, folding the letter into an envelope.

"I think you have a better chance of hearing from Eleanor Roosevelt."

"Oh, Flash, don't be such a pessimist," I say, writing out the address. "Let's just wait and see."

It's up to you, Bill. We're still waiting.

About the Author

LESLÉA NEWMAN's writing has appeared in a wide variety
of publications, ranging from *Common Lives/Lesbian Lives* to
Seventeen magazine. She has published more than twenty
books for adults and children, including *The Femme Mystique,
A Letter to Harvey Milk, Every Woman's Dream, Sweet Dark
Places,* and *Heather Has Two Mommies.* Four of her books have
been Lambda Literary Award finalists. Forthcoming books
include a collection of poetry, *Still Life With Buddy,* and an
anthology titled *Pillow Talk: Lesbian Stories Between the Covers.*